AN EYE TO THE CROWN

A lifestyle for ultimate victory

An Eye to the
CROWN

A LIFESTYLE FOR ULTIMATE VICTORY

BOLA OGEDENGBE

AN EYE TO THE CROWN A Lifestyle for Ultimate Victory

Copyright © 2016 Bolanle Ogedengbe

All rights reserved. No part of this publication may be reproduced, stored in a retrieval system, distributed, or transmitted in any form or by any means, including photocopying, recording, or other electronic or mechanical methods – except for brief quotations in printed reviews – without the prior written permission of the publisher.

All Scripture quotations, unless otherwise indicated, are taken from The Holy Bible, New International Version® NIV®. Copyright © 1973, 1978, 1984 by International Bible Society®. Used by permission.

ISBN 979-10-95039-04-4 9791095039013

Dépôt légal July 2016

Scripture quotations marked HCSB®, are taken from the Holman Christian Standard Bible®, Copyright © 1999, 2000, 2002, 2003, 2009 by Holman Bible Publishers. Used by permission. HCSB® is a federally registered trademark of Holman Bible Publishers.

Dedication

To my father, Samuel Adebisi Ogedengbe ... the first to nurture my love for books, language, and all things literary.

Remembering the many hours spent buried in his books. Today I minister and pastor from my base in Paris, and all those years ago it was his Linguaphone language CDs that first kindled my fascination for the French language.

Contents

	Acknowledgements	ix
	Prologue	x
	Preface	xi
1.	Go Tell	1
2.	Worship and Fellowship	35
3.	Read	55
4.	Pray	93
5.	Be baptised	113
6.	Receive Holy Spirit baptism	127
7.	Serve	149
8.	Fast	179
9.	Give	203
10.	Change	241

Bibliography   259
About the Author   260
Other books by Author   261

Acknowledgements

Praise, thanks, and gratitude to my Lord and Saviour Jesus Christ. He called, saved, and empowered me to fulfil a glorious destiny. Everything that is right is right because of Him.

My thanks go to all the friends and family who gave unstinting support to this project. Wale and Uche, for their contributions; my family for the moral and prayer support; my nephew Nelson, whose enchantment with the book-writing process caused much merriment. I hope I have inspired him.

Prologue

'Do you not know that in a race all the runners run, but only one gets the prize? Run in such a way as to get the prize.

Everyone who competes in the games goes into strict training, conducts himself temperately and restricts himself in all things. They do it to get a crown that will not last; but we do it to get a crown that will last forever.

Therefore, I do not run like a man running aimlessly; I do not fight like a man beating the air.

No, I beat my body and make it my slave that after I have preached to others, I myself will not be disqualified for the prize'
    (1 Corinthians 9.24-27).

Preface

'In the same way, faith by itself, if it is not accompanied by action, is dead' (James 2.17).

Egg-and-spoon race, sack race, the 100-metre dash (on the odd occasion) – those were my contributions to the athletic endeavours of my secondary school. Needless to say, I was not the school's star athlete. The 100-metre dash I do not ever remember winning; I do remember ending it panting, out of breath. The daily games period served a more useful purpose. It was a time for chatting, lying on the grass with friends and indulging in non-energy, non-muscle-building activities. And although I still valiantly pursued other sporting activities – lawn tennis for instance – it was, alas with no memorable results. Some of the girls seemed to fly when they hit the track. Others displayed remarkable endurance covering several laps with relative ease and speed. It befell the rest of us to sit in the audience and gape and gasp in amazement. No doubt you already get my point. Athletic prowess is not equally distributed; not all can excel, nor are they expected to.

The Bible compares the Christian life to running a race. Unlike the aforementioned races, however, in this race all the runners are equally enabled to win. All are *expected* to win, though not all do. In the passage below, Paul the Apostle points out that not all the runners who compete in a race win the prize. Then he challenges us to run in such a way that we will win the prize.

> 'Do you not know that in a race all the runners run, but only one gets the prize? Run in such a way as to get the prize. Everyone who competes in the game goes into strict training. They do it to get a crown that will not last; but we do it to get a crown that will last forever' (1 Corinthians 9.24-25).

In the light of this statement from God's Word, a question that must be paramount in the mind of every believer is this: 'How do we run this race to ensure that we will win the prize?' This volume seeks to answer that question. It aims to give you a few pointers on how to run this race. You are as well endowed as anyone else to do so successfully. There is method, effort, and substance to the Christian life.

> 'Therefore I do not run like a man running aimlessly; I do not fight like a man beating the air. No, I beat my body and make it my slave so that after I have preached to others, I

myself will not be disqualified for the prize' (1 Corinthians 9.26-27).

Picture yourself at the starting blocks with a line of runners, all of whom look promising. As the race advances, performance levels begin to differ. On reaching the finishing line, you find that many have dropped off, while some come limping in on all fours. Finally, others – I would hope you included – run majestically to the end and are crowned. Talent is not all there is to the story. Some people excelled because they applied themselves more to their training and preparation and showed more discipline. When you apply yourself to training, preparation, and discipline, the success of your Christian life will be evident. You make the choices, not God alone, so make the right choices.

In Christ you have received a new identity and new life. Now you are setting off on the Christian race. Before you are two roads. Road One leads to a life of beauty and excellence in Christ, a life of transformation, deep communion with God, and fulfilment of divine purpose. Road Two speaks of mediocrity, haziness, and deep spiritual dissatisfaction. I have no doubt which road you will choose.

What kind of athlete will you be? Casual and indifferent? Or serious and disciplined?

Faith, we are told, without corresponding action is dead. On the first road, you will take specific actions that help you to consistently imbibe and practice God's Word to the point where it will refashion you, and displace your old identity and conduct. The resultant actions will cause you to enjoy Christ to the fullest. You will, freely and gratefully, fulfil all your obligations to the One who has been such an amazing benefactor to you.

Simply put, there is a lifestyle incumbent on anyone who has professed faith in Christ and embraced His new identity. It is a lifestyle that will lead to transformation and fulfilment of divine purpose. That is what this volume is about, coming hot on the heels of the first volume on your new identity in Christ.

What, then, do we do on a daily basis to fulfil the divine purpose of God in saving us? Come with me as we examine a ten-point plan to spiritual excellence.

1

Go Tell

"Some men's ambition is art. Some men's ambition is fame. Some men's ambition is gold. My ambition is the souls of men."

(William Booth in King Edward VII's autograph book, 1904)

*

> 'Go tell it on the mountain
> Over the hill and everywhere
> Go tell it on the mountain
> That Jesus Christ saved you.'

Remember the old spiritual, albeit slightly altered? That is more or less what Jesus said to a person whose life had been totally transformed by his contact with Jesus, a man from a region called Gadara. The poor fellow was severely afflicted by the devil and lived more or less like an outcast. When Jesus arrived, the evil spirits inside the man resented His presence and spoke out through the man. Jesus set him free, to the utter astonishment of the townspeople. At a loss as to how to handle this dramatic turn of events, they asked Jesus to take Himself and His strange powers elsewhere. As Jesus was leaving, the man, now in his right mind, asked Jesus if He could go with Him. Jesus declined and instead told him to go back home and tell of all that God had done for him.

Your encounter with Jesus may not have been that visibly dramatic, but the spiritual dynamics were no less earth-shaking. You have passed from death to life. You are born again, not of *perishable seed, but of imperishable, through the living and enduring word of God* (1 Peter 1.23). God saw you heading for an eternity in utter darkness and He reached out to rescue you. We – you and I – were the 'others' excluded from grace, but He has now included us in His family. We who were not a people are now called the people of God, members of the household of faith. It is nothing short of mind boggling. Having received this great grace, Jesus commands us to not keep it to ourselves, but to go and tell others so they can receive the same. We call it witnessing, sharing the gospel.

As you begin this race, let witnessing be one of the founding principles of your life. It is an honour and an amazing privilege to be chosen by the Lord to speak for Him to mankind. Some people take to it with ease, with great joy and excitement. Some – for social, cultural, or personal reasons – may feel intimidated and unsuited for the job. However, that is a handicap that can and should be overcome. I know many people who were initially unsure of what to say, or of their ability to say, who today take great delight in telling all who will hear about the Lord Jesus.

MANY HAVE NOT BEEN TOLD

In a film on the early ministry of Hudson Taylor, the great 19th century missionary to China, he is depicted in a scene conversing with a Chinese convert. The convert enthused about the peace and joy he had found since coming to the Lord. He described how he had sought this peace with God in his previous religious observance, but had not found it. Then he asked this question, 'In your country, how long have people known the gospel?' Hudson Taylor replied, 'hundreds of years'. The young Chinese convert looked at him in stunned surprise and said, 'And you are just now coming to tell us?'

Unfortunately, many today have still not been told. In Hudson Taylor's day, the sea voyage to China took over one month, yet he and many others went. Why? Because they cared about the souls of men. Because God's way of saving humanity is to have another human tell them about Jesus' offer of salvation. And as they are told, the power of God works in them to bring them to faith. That is how you came to Jesus. Yet in many parts of the world – possibly including where you live – people are not being told, though there are people in their neighbourhood and city who 'know the gospel'. Too many are still in the dark, even on the streets we walk every day.

Once I spoke to someone at some length about the Lord. They looked at me in disbelief and quipped, 'If it was so, surely it would be widespread knowledge'. In our city, as we witness, we repeatedly encounter people in their 20s and 30s who have never had a conversation about Jesus with anyone who knew the gospel. It is quite possible that your neighbours, friends, and co-workers may never have been told.

If that shocks you, consider that some people dutifully attend church services every week and have not been told either. They have little or no understanding of who Jesus is, why He came, what He offers them, and why they need

Him. I was one of these people. I grew up in church and I even sang in the choir for a brief spell; however, I did not hear the gospel until I went to university ... and would you believe it, it struck me as ridiculous? I had no idea that was what Christianity taught.

There are other people who may think Jesus is one of many gods, and would willingly add Him to their pantheon. Still others see Him as a great prophet, but not as God made flesh. You will encounter them all.

None of these opinions about Jesus leads to salvation. Lovely though these people are, they are separated from God and will remain so unless someone takes it upon themselves to tell them. Perhaps you also went for years without anyone telling you the truth about Jesus. Aren't you glad they finally did? So what is so amazing about witnessing?

WHAT IS SO AMAZING ABOUT WITNESSING?

It is an invitation to life

To witness is to issue an invitation to people to come to Jesus. Without it, they will remain dead in their sins and in darkness. They remain lost. Without it, they will be deprived of the opportunity to know God. That is why people like Paul the Apostle travelled thousands of kilometres going from place to place telling those He encountered about Jesus. He knew that unless someone told them, they would have no opportunity to believe.

The same is true today. That is why the Scriptures say in Romans 10.17 that 'Consequently, faith comes from hearing the message, and the message is heard through the word of Christ.' The Word of God spoken to them is the source of understanding, revelation, and faith. You have the privilege of speaking that word and seeing a life changed forever. Think about it.

It is an act of love

Witnessing is a great opportunity to demonstrate our love for Jesus. Why? Because Jesus wants to save. Since we know that He makes His call to salvation through *people*, we choose to become those people through whom He does so because we love Him and want to please Him.

Do you know that the Bible says that there is joy in the presence of the angels in heaven when one person comes to Jesus? Isn't that just astounding? Doesn't it make you want to be the one God uses to trigger joy in heaven? Imagine the joy of the hosts of heaven, the joy of the Son of God as He sees His sacrifice bearing fruit in the lives of people through your agency!

The coming of Jesus to our sin-torn world was an act of love beyond compare. He paid dearly to make salvation freely available to all. It cost Him His glory, it cost Him His earthly life, it cost Him His honour and dignity on the earth; and now the deed is accomplished and the door is open to every man. I have walked through that door, and so have you. And He summons others to do the same, for their sake. He summons your friends, colleagues, family members, every person on the face of the earth. And He asks, as He said within earshot of a man called Isaiah, 'Who will go?'

When we are thinking straight, we do what Isaiah did. We ourselves beg for the privilege to be the one who 'will go'.

Isaiah spoke up and said, 'Here am I. Send me!' We also say the same, just to say thank you, to say, 'I love you Lord, and I am grateful'. The work is His, the power is His, the saving is His, but the speaking is ours. It is a most extraordinary privilege to be able to speak words to people that Jesus will use to open their hearts to receive Him.

It is also an act of love towards the people to whom we witness. There is no greater gift to offer a person than the gift of eternal life and reconciliation with the Father. It is humbling to think that it is in our power to help someone avoid hell. We do not save them, but God uses the things we say and do to save them. I definitely want to be a part of giving people the offer of life. Think about it. All the people who spoke to you about Jesus exercised that power. And they are a part of the reason why you are reading this book, secure in the knowledge that after death you will not go to hell. Shall we purchase expensive treasures for people and omit to offer them, at no cost, the most valuable (and, indeed, the only truly valuable treasure of all) life in

Jesus? God can use you to change someone's whole existence and their eternal destination. What else is so amazing about witnessing?

To witness is to discharge our duties

What duties? Our ambassadorial duties. We took on, in the new birth, the right to citizenship and the role of ambassador in the kingdom of God. An ambassador is one who represents the interests of his country of origin and who speaks on behalf of and defends the interests of his country of origin. He contributes to enhancing its power and influence. That is our role on the earth, to represent Jesus in a foreign world and contribute to enhancing the scope and influence of God's kingdom in the earth.

The Apostle Paul, inspired by the Holy Spirit, waxed lyrical in that remarkable passage in the second letter to the Corinthian church where he says:

> 'We are therefore Christ's ambassadors , as though God were making his appeal through us. We implore you on Christ's behalf: "Be reconciled to God" (2 Corinthians 5.20).

Jesus commands us to do it

When you witness, you are obeying Jesus. When you don't, you are not. It is that simple. Jesus wants to save people. He has commanded those of us who belong to Him, who have received salvation, to go out and bring others to Him. He said to go to the whole world and preach the gospel to them, make them committed followers of Jesus, and teach them to obey Him. We call it the Great Commission. It was the one mandate Jesus left His disciples at His departure. It is the greatest task of the church and the jewel of all Christian endeavour.

To obey and to worship is also about bringing others to obey and worship Him. It is about causing more and more people to recognise the astounding sacrifice of Jesus and honour Him. And when you begin to see them come to Jesus, the thrill and joy is indescribable. The greatest joy, of course, is knowing how much joy it gives the Lord.

By now, you are probably eager to know how to trigger this indescribable joy, but first, one final point on why witnessing is so marvellous.

It is a huge blessing to the one witnessing

When you talk about Jesus to other people, He becomes more precious to you. In sharing about what Jesus has done and who He is, your knowledge of and love for Him grows, as well as your gratitude towards Him. You step into a beautiful process of progressive revelation. The more precious Jesus is to you, the more beautiful your life becomes because He is the sweet savour of your existence.

Another corollary of witnessing is great joy, a God-given joy. First, there is the sheer joy that comes from talking about the Lord. Then, there is also the fact that what you are doing is pleasing to God, thus the Holy Spirit blesses you and you are filled with joy.

Some have to conquer their timidity, some their brashness; all must learn to follow the Holy Spirit. Expect tough times. At times, you will face opposition and persecution. At other times, it is your own reluctance to obey God that will cause you trouble. The Apostles took it all in their stride. After being threatened, they returned to the other believers filled with great joy. God wants to toughen us, and the succeeding chapters of this book show the different spiritual disciplines that will strengthen us and make us spiritually powerful.

When you witness, you know you are pleasing God. The Scriptures celebrate soulwinners and call them wise. So be wise and expect God to bless you more and more as you go out and talk to people about God.

WHAT DO I DO?

A few pointers.

Tell your story

The first thing many people do is tell their story; they tell friends and family what happened to them – what Jesus did for them. Why not start there? Tell your story. Yes, tell everybody what happened to you. Let's do a quick quiz:

- When you watch a good movie, do you discuss it spontaneously?

- When you come back from holiday, do you start showing your pictures and holding forth about all the places you visited?

- When you have a baby, do you share your stories and bore even childless people with your endless baby pictures?

If you ticked yes to at least one of those boxes, you are a natural personal witnessing expert. So tell your story. Tell everybody you are a follower of Christ now, and tell them what difference it has made to your life. Some people will rejoice with you; others may think you have finally lost it. They had been expecting it for some years now, and now it has happened. They will smile quietly and think 'poor soul'. Some will be curious and ask to know more. Some, though interested, will wait to see if it will last before they accept it as genuine. Some will argue for a while and then follow you into the faith.

Whatever you do, *do not be silent.*

Explain the change

Some time ago, I spoke to a young person who had recently committed her life to the Lord. At work people had noticed the change in her conduct. Situations would come up where people would expect her to fly off the handle, but she would just move on. Once a person was very rude to her and she simply spoke firmly and let them go.

A colleague who witnessed the scene was stunned, saying, 'You let them go just like that?'

'Yes.'

'You have changed!'

Most of us receive such comments when we first come to the Lord. Something changes radically that people notice. Seize the opportunity to tell them why. Many people just smile and acknowledge the change when others comment; you do not want to do that. You want to use it as an entry point. Explain why. Sometimes you even get pointed questions like, 'What happened to you? You are so different.' Yet some Christians still don't say why!

Do tell. Tell them, 'I gave my life to Jesus and He is changing me radically.' They cannot deny the change; they mentioned it. They may huff at your reason, but they will think it over again.

Among the most visited pages on our website are the testimony pages where people talk about their encounter with the Lord and how He changed their lives. Even people who do not know them are keen to hear about the change. So, pray tell.

Let your life speak

It's what we call walking the walk and not just talking the talk. The rest of this book will be devoted to telling you even more things to do, just in case you are like I was when I came to the Lord. All I intended to do was receive Jesus.

Well, I did pray and read the Bible. In fact, I devoured it. However, joining a local church was out of the question, as were many other healthy things I am now recommending to you, things that Jesus would have us do.

What is my point? Simple! Your new life should lead to a changed life, inside and outside. Live it fully. People will be watching you like hawks. Your credibility will depend more on your doing the right thing than on your saying it. Your friends may laugh at you because you change your habits, but if you don't, they will never take your faith seriously. Not only that, but they almost certainly will not come to the Lord through you.

It's interesting, isn't it? You may first have to displease them to reach them for the Lord. If you continue to live as before, (that would be odd if you were really saved), they may slap you on the back and say you are a good sport; you are not like so-and-so who got religious and went weird on them. However, what they mean is that you are a hypocrite and they like your hypocrisy because it does not challenge them.

> **Your friends may laugh at you because you change your habits, but if you don't, they will never take your faith seriously.**

However, witnessing with your life does not preclude actually speaking to people about salvation through Christ. People will often notice a particular characteristic about you and comment on it. It gives you a chance to tell them about Jesus. That is worth its weight in gold. However, for many believers, it means not talking about Jesus at all; being a 'good person' is sufficient. Indeed, 'I am witnessing with my life' is the default cowardly position of many believers who never share the gospel.

Many years ago, I accidentally discovered that a professional colleague was a Christian. So we talked about reaching her entourage with the gospel. Her response? No, there is no need to actually speak to people; she was witnessing with her life. What that means is that she said absolutely nothing to people. She just lived a wonderful Christian life and expected that at some point people would see how great Christianity is and come to the Lord.

Are you thinking that sounds like a great idea? It's not. In fact, it's a terrible idea. Some people will never ask. Besides, you have to have a totally inflated idea of your own goodness to stake the eternal salvation of people on their noticing it so strongly they want to follow in your footsteps. Not a single one of us is that amazing. Even if we were to be perfection incarnated, like Jesus, surely we would still need to speak to some people. Jesus did. Obedience to God is our first duty as a Christian, so we must live right and also employ language in sharing the gospel.

Learn and share the substance of the gospel

You have the opportunity to start on the right footing. Learn the gospel. Go beyond what Jesus did for you personally and begin to study the different ramifications of His life and sacrifice. Learn at least the basics of the redemption story – sin, separation, Christ, redemption, reconciliation, etc. You do not want to be like people who, after many years in the faith, still cannot articulate the message of the gospel clearly; they are gospel illiterates.

Tell people in simple words about their condition as sinners, their need for a Saviour, why Jesus came, what He did, and what He is still doing now. Tell them about the cross and the resurrection; tell them that Jesus took their pain and punishment. Tell them about the promise of the new birth, forgiveness, joy, peace with God, etc.

One young man I know was speaking to a co-worker about the Lord and the co-worker was stunned when he spoke of forgiveness. He could not fathom that in the Christian faith you were supposed to forgive people who do you harm. He blurted out in astonishment 'Your faith is bizarre'.

What are you to say to such a person? Explain that the Christian is expected to forgive and is able to forgive *because he himself has been forgiven.* I told the young man he needed to tell his co-worker about the cross. He must explain to him that Jesus became our substitute; He was wounded and bruised for our sins, and forgave us. Who then are we to hold unforgiveness against another?

Pray for them, in particular, for the sick

Tell them about healing. If they need healing, pray for them to be healed. Healing in answer to prayer is a great testimony to non-believers that God loves them. One powerful way to touch people is to pray for their problems. When God answers, it often opens their hearts to God. You can lay hands on the sick and pray for them to be healed.

Jesus is so loving; you can believe Him for their healing. Study divine healing and get an understanding of God's goodness to heal. There is a young man of my acquaintance who became a Christian after receiving healing. He had strenuously rebuffed efforts to win him to Christ, but he agreed to attend a healing service. He received prayer, God healed him and he committed his life to Christ.

Let me tell you a secret. The more you think about these truths, the more they enthral you, the more your understanding and revelation grows, and the more unshakeable and convincing you become. The Holy Spirit will teach you. He will speak through you. I pray that you will be very fruitful. Fruitful doesn't mean that you are birthing apples and oranges; it means seeing many people come to Jesus through you.

A few more pointers

Not everybody will agree.

Never be discouraged when a person says no. Besides, you never know when they will bow the knee to Jesus. That person may be as I was. Many years ago, Christians would witness to me continually, mostly people who I did not know personally. Very few people in my entourage were Christians. I rebuffed all such effort systematically, but their words stuck. At some point, I felt compelled to find out if there was anything to this 'Jesus thing'.

Many years later, I spoke to one of those people who had witnessed to me in the past and borne the brunt of my sharp tongue. I had the privilege of encouraging them in their walk with God as they had in the meantime cooled somewhat in their faith.

Answer people's questions.

The first thing to know is that you must develop a love for questions. Many people ask questions to be argumentative, but most people ask because they are pondering, which means they are interested. Even if they are being argumentative, it still gives you an opportunity to share the gospel.

Once I was discussing salvation with someone who honours Jesus as a prophet, but totally refuses the biblical presentation of Jesus as the Saviour and Son of God. He had been extremely argumentative and, at one point, pugnaciously challenged me to tell my side of the story, confident that the biblical account was wobbly and untenable. His challenge was a godsend. I launched into a very detailed presentation of the redemption story – beginning with the fall, through the covenants, to the prophets and the promise of Messiah, all the way to Jesus. I explained the nature of Jesus, the Cross, the Resurrection, and individual salvation. Since he had asked, he had to hear me through.

At the end, somewhat subdued, he replied, 'so that is your story.'

I confidently replied, 'yes, that is *the* story.' I doubt that man had ever heard that level of the gospel presentation. I went on my way happy that the seed had been sown generously.

That was an easy one. Sometimes, when you do not know the answer or you had never encountered such a question before, even as they speak, ask the Holy Spirit for help inwardly. You will often find yourself receiving understanding and giving answers you would never have thought up yourself. At such times you literally want to press 'record' so you can hear it again. Many times it is when people have asked me difficult questions that I have grown in revelation as I received insight from the Holy Spirit.

If you have no insight, tell them you cannot answer that one, but you will get back to them on it. Do not pretend you know everything. Go back and study the Word of

God. If it is related to Christian apologetics, study apologetics.

The truth is that you do not need to know everything to believe in Jesus or to win people to Jesus. There is no one question or hidden secret that, upon discovery, will negate faith in Christ. Nor is there any philosophical or scientific question that must absolutely be answered for people to believe in Christ. Of course, you must study to learn more and be able to give a reason for the hope that you have, as the Scriptures say. Remember, though, that Jesus is real and is who He says He is; He is not going away just because you face a philosophical conundrum. Read this passage attentively; it is very instructive.

> 'For the message of the cross is foolishness to those who are perishing, but to us who are being saved it is the power of God. For it is written: "I will destroy the wisdom of the wise; the intelligence of the intelligent I will frustrate." Where is the wise man? Where is the scholar? Where is the philosopher of this age? Has not God made foolish the wisdom of the world?' (1 Corinthians 1.18-20).

What to avoid

Christians

No, not all of them ... just the ones who want to argue over doctrine while you are trying to win people to Jesus. You will find, unfortunately, that many believers are apt to split hairs over their pet doctrines. They are apt to deride other churches and fuss a great deal over little, and are often little inclined to reach out to the lost. Welcome to the kingdom. When you meet someone like that who turns out to be a Christian, love them, move on, and hunt out a true heathen. Don't argue with them about the order or length of service, boast that your choir is the best, or waste time debating any other silly things some Christians think are so important.

Contention

Excessive argumentation is detrimental to evangelism. You end up rubbing people up the wrong way and they cease to listen to you. Some people just want to fight, so don't indulge them. The truth is, believers are God's hand and God's voice in their generation. You have something precious that the people you meet desperately need, whether or not they are aware of it. But don't force it on them or think that unless you win the argument, God will look bad. God can defend His own honour. Take it from someone who used to trounce Christians in arguments.

Make up your mind not to settle into comfortable church life focusing on how much God can do for you. Live the exciting life of letting God do things through you, things like saving people, healing, setting people free, etc. That is the good life par excellence.

How to begin

Pray. Ask the Holy Spirit to guide you and lead people to you.

Begin with your friends, family, colleagues, and schoolmates. They are the people you see the most, plus (in the case of families), they are stuck with you. They will not drop you like a hot potato because you are a believer. (Well, they should not, although some do.) No doubt they are also the people you are most eager to see converted.

Ask God daily to bring people your way. Tell anyone who will listen, on the mountain top, over the hill and everywhere, remember? You will begin to see openings in conversations and notice people coming to ask you questions. Jump in unashamedly and talk about Jesus. It is to their benefit.

Pray daily for the people you have witnessed to and ask God to make you a joyful soul winner. Pray that the Holy Spirit will work on their hearts to give them understanding of the gospel and conviction of sin. Don't go by the supposed indifference of some and the apparent enthusiasm of others. Entrust them into God's hands by praying fervently for them.

We cannot possibly say all there is to be said about winning souls to Jesus, but know this one thing: it should be your primary Christian activity besides prayer and worship. As a postscript, I leave you with a vision received by William Booth, (1829-1912) founder of the Salvation

Army. It galvanised him into a ministry of soulwinning that touched millions of people. I pray it will bless you.

A VISION OF THE LOST

by William Booth. (1829-1912)

On one of my recent journeys, as I gazed from the coach window, I was led into a train of thought concerning the condition of the multitudes around me. They were living carelessly in the most open and shameless rebellion against God, without a thought for their eternal welfare. As I looked out of the window, I seemed to see them all… millions of people all around me given up to their drink and their pleasure, their dancing and their music, their business and their anxieties, their politics and their troubles. Ignorant – willfully ignorant in many cases – and in other instances knowing all about the truth and not caring at all. But all of them, the whole mass of them, sweeping on and up in their blasphemies and devilries to the Throne of God. While my mind was thus engaged, I had a vision.

I saw a dark and stormy ocean. Over it the black clouds hung heavily; through them every now and then vivid lightning flashed and loud thunder rolled, while the winds moaned, and the waves rose and foamed, towered and broke, only to rise and foam, tower and break again.

In that ocean I thought I saw myriads of poor human beings plunging and floating, shouting and shrieking, cursing and struggling and drowning; and as they cursed and screamed they rose and shrieked again, and then some sank to rise no more.

And I saw out of this dark angry ocean, a mighty rock that rose up with its summit towering high above the black clouds that overhung the stormy sea. And all around the base of this great rock I saw a vast platform. Onto this platform, I saw with delight a number of the poor struggling, drowning wretches continually climbing out of the angry ocean. And I saw that a few of those who were already safe on the platform were helping the poor creatures still in the angry waters to reach the place of safety.

On looking more closely I found a number of those who had been rescued, industriously working and scheming by ladders, ropes, boats and other means more effective, to deliver the poor strugglers out of the sea. Here and there were some who actually jumped into the water, regardless of the consequences in their passion to "rescue the perishing." And I hardly know which gladdened me the most – the sight of the poor drowning people climbing onto the rocks reaching a place of safety, or the devotion and self-sacrifice of those whose whole being was wrapped up in the effort for their deliverance.

As I looked on, I saw that the occupants of that platform were quite a mixed company. That is, they were divided into different "sets" or classes, and they occupied themselves with different pleasures and employments. But only a very few of them seemed to make it their business to get the people out of the sea.

But what puzzled me most was the fact that though all of them had been rescued at one time or another from the ocean, nearly everyone seemed to have forgotten all about it. Anyway, it seemed the memory of its darkness and danger no longer troubled them at all. And what seemed equally strange and perplexing to me was that these people did not even seem to have any care – that is any agonizing care – about the poor perishing ones who were struggling and drowning right before their very eyes… many of whom were their own husbands and wives, brothers and sisters and even their own children.

Now this astonishing unconcern could not have been the result of ignorance or lack of knowledge, because they lived right there in full sight of it all and even talked about it sometimes. Many even went regularly to hear lectures and sermons in which the awful state of these poor drowning creatures was described.

I have always said that the occupants of this platform were engaged in different pursuits and pastimes. Some of them were absorbed day and night in trading and business in order to make gain, storing up their savings in boxes, safes and the like.

Many spent their time in amusing themselves with growing flowers on the side of the rock, others in painting pieces of cloth or in playing music, or in dressing themselves up in different styles and walking about to be admired. Some occupied themselves chiefly in eating and drinking, others were taken up with arguing about the poor drowning creatures that had already been rescued.

But the thing to me that seemed the most amazing was that those on the platform to whom He called, who heard His voice and felt that they ought to obey it – at least they said they did – those who confessed to love Him much were in full sympathy with Him in the task He had undertaken – who worshipped Him or who professed to do so – were so taken up with their trades and professions, their money saving and pleasures, their families and circles, their religions and arguments about it, and their preparation for going to the mainland, that they did not listen to the cry that came to them from this Wonderful Being who had Himself gone down into the sea. Anyway, if they heard it they did not heed it. They did not care. And so the multitude went on right before them struggling and shrieking and drowning in the darkness.

And then I saw something that seemed to me even more strange than anything that had gone on before in this strange vision. I saw that some of these people on the platform whom this Wonderful Being had called to, wanting them to come and help Him in His difficult task of saving these perishing creatures, were always praying and crying out to Him to come to them!

Some wanted Him to come and stay with them, and spend His time and strength in making them happier. Others wanted Him to come and take away various doubts and misgivings they had concerning the truth of some letters He had written them. Some wanted Him to come and make them feel more secure on the rock – so secure that they would be quite sure that they should never slip off again into the ocean. Numbers of others wanted Him to make them feel quite certain that they would really get off the rock and onto the mainland someday: because as a matter of fact, it was well known that some had walked so carelessly as to loose their footing, and had fallen back again into the stormy waters.

So these people used to meet and get up as high on the rock as they could, and looking towards the mainland (where they thought the Great Being was) they would cry out, "Come to us! Come and help us!" And all the while He was down (by His Spirit) among the poor struggling, drowning creatures in the angry deep, with His arms around them trying to drag them out, and looking up – oh! so longingly but all in vain – to those on the rock, crying to them with His voice all hoarse from calling, "Come to Me! Come, and help Me!

And then I understood it all. It was plain enough. The sea was the ocean of life – the sea of real, actual human existence. That lightning was the gleaming of piercing truth coming from Jehovah's Throne. That thunder was the distant echoing of the wrath of God. Those multitudes of people shrieking, struggling and agonizing in the stormy sea, were the thousands and thousands of poor harlots and harlot-makers, of drunkards and drunkard makers, of thieves, liars, blasphemers and ungodly people of every kindred, tongue and nation.

Oh what a black sea it was! And oh, what multitudes of rich and poor, ignorant and educated were there. They were all so unalike in their outward circumstances and conditions, yet all alike in one thing – all sinners before God – all held by, and holding onto, some iniquity, fascinated by some idol, the slaves of some devilish lust, and ruled by the foul fiend from the bottomless pit!

"All alike in one thing?" No, all alike in two things – not only the same in their wickedness but, unless rescued, the same in their sinking, sinking... down, down, down... to the same terrible doom. That great sheltering rock represented Calvary, the place where Jesus had died for them. And the people on it were those who had been rescued. The way they used their energies, gifts and time represented the occupations and amusements of those who professed to be saved from sin and hell – followers of the Lord Jesus Christ. The handful of fierce, determined ones, who were risking their own lives in saving the perishing were true soldiers of the cross of Jesus. That Mighty Being who was calling to them from the midst of the angry waters was the Son of God, "the same yesterday, today and forever" who is still struggling and interceding to save the dying multitudes about us from this terrible doom of damnation, and whose voice can be heard above the music, machinery, and noise of life, calling on the rescued to come and help Him save the world.

My friends in Christ, you are rescued from the waters, you are on the rock, He is in the dark sea calling on you to come to Him and help Him. Will you go? Look for yourselves. The surging sea of life, crowded with perishing multitudes rolls up to the very spot on which you stand. Leaving the vision, I now come to speak of the fact – a fact that is as real as the Bible, as real as the Christ who hung upon the cross, as real as the judgment day will be, and as real as the heaven and hell that will follow it.

Look! Don't be deceived by appearances – men and things are not what they seem. All who are not on the rock are in the sea! Look at them from the standpoint of the great White Throne, and what a sight you have! Jesus Christ, the Son of God is, through His Spirit, in the midst of this dying multitude, struggling to save them. And He is calling on you to jump into the sea – to go right away to His side and help Him in the holy strife. Will you jump? That is, will you go to His feet and place yourself absolutely at His disposal?

A young Christian once came to me, and told me that for some time she had been giving the Lord her profession and prayers and money, but now she wanted to give Him her life. She wanted to go right into the fight. In other words, she wanted to go to His assistance in the sea. As when a man from the shore, seeing another struggling in the water, takes off those outer garments that would hinder his efforts and leaps to the rescue, so will you who still linger on the bank, thinking and singing and praying about the poor perishing souls, lay aside your shame, your pride, your cares about other people's opinions, your love of ease and all the selfish loves that have kept you back for so long, and rush to the rescue of this multitude of dying men and women.

Does the surging sea look dark and dangerous? Unquestionably it is so. There is no doubt that the leap for you, as for everyone who takes it, means difficulty and scorn and suffering. For you it may mean more than this. It may mean death. He who beckons you from the sea however, knows what it will mean – and knowing, He still calls to you and bids to you to come.

You must do it! You cannot hold back. You have enjoyed yourself in Christianity long enough. You have had pleasant feelings, pleasant songs, pleasant meetings, pleasant prospects. There has been much of human happiness, much clapping of hands and shouting of praises – very much of heaven on earth.

Now then, go to God and tell Him you are prepared as much as necessary to turn your back upon it all, and that you are willing to spend the rest of your days struggling in the midst of these perishing multitudes, whatever it may cost you.

You must do it. With the light that is now broken in upon your mind and the call that is now sounding in your ears, and the beckoning hands that are now before your eyes, you have no alternative. To go down among the perishing crowds is your duty. Your happiness from now on will consist in sharing their misery, your ease in sharing their pain, your crown in helping them to bear their cross, and your heaven in going into the very jaws of hell to rescue them.

*

Scriptures for meditation

John 3.16 – 'For God so loved the world, that he gave his one and only Son, that whoever believes in him should not perish, but have eternal life.'

Acts 1.8 – 'But you will receive power when the Holy Spirit comes on you: and you will be my witnesses in Jerusalem, and in all Judea and Samaria, and to the ends of the earth.'

Matthew 28.18-19 – 'Then Jesus came to them and said, "All authority in heaven and on earth has been given to me. Therefore go and make disciples of all nations, baptising them in the name of the Father and of the Son and of the Holy Spirit,"'

Romans 1.16 – 'I am not ashamed of the gospel, because it is the power of God for the salvation of everyone who believes: first for the Jew, then for the Gentile.'

Romans 10.17 – 'Consequently faith comes from hearing the message, and the message is heard through the word of Christ.'

Mark 16.15 – 'He said to them, "Go into all the world and preach the good news to all creation."'

1 Peter 3.15 – 'But in your hearts set apart Christ as Lord. Always be prepared to give an answer to everyone who asks you to give the reason for the hope that you have. But do this with gentleness and respect,'

[See also: Acts 2.37-38; Matthew 5.16; Isaiah 43.10; Colossians 4.2-6; Acts 17.1-3; Acts 16.13; Acts 19.8-9; John 4.29]

*

Points to ponder

- Having received this great grace, Jesus commands us to not keep it to ourselves, but to go and tell others so they can receive the same.

- Make up your mind not to settle into comfortable church life focusing on how much God can do for you.

- Never be discouraged when a person says no. Besides, you never know when they will bow the knee to Jesus.

Discussion questions

1. Why is it important to witness once you are born again?
2. What are some of the means by which you can witness effectively?
3. Why is it not always enough to tell your story?
4. What conclusions would you draw from William Booth's amazing vision?

Prayer

Father, thank You for saving me.

Please open my eyes to the condition of the people around me who do not know You. Give me boldness to preach the gospel. Give me a passion for souls. Make me an effective soulwinner. In Jesus' name. Amen.

2

Worship and Fellowship

> "Christianity is not a purely intellectual, internal faith. It can only be lived in community."
>
> Philip Yancey,
> (Church: Why Bother?:
> My Personal Pilgrimage)

*

'They devoted themselves to the apostles' teaching and to the fellowship, to the breaking of bread and to prayer' (Acts 2.42).

A man receives a divine revelation. On the strength of it, he changes course and heads, along with his companions for a continent hitherto untouched by the gospel. On arrival in the principal city of the region, they know no one, but quickly seek out those who would be inclined to hear about God. They go to a well known place of prayer, the man finds some women, and he speaks to them. Several persons are touched. One in particular is so radically affected by this message that she opens her home to the strangers, and they accept her hospitality.

They continue their work and they see many come to faith. However, they end up falling foul of some influential people hell-bent on stopping them. They are locked up in prison, undaunted and defiant. Through miraculous circumstances, they are delivered, but they must go elsewhere. However, on departure, they are able to leave behind a group of believers, an assembly meeting regularly for worship and for fellowship. The place is Philippi and the man is Paul the Apostle.

From Philippi, Paul and his companions journey onward to the next place and the next and the next, until the end of his ministry. In every place, they win souls. Though culture and circumstance may differ, in each instance they organise the believers into a group. The group is meant to gather for worship and fellowship, with clearly identified leaders to care for the flock. We call such a group of believers a church. Their goal was not simply to bring individuals to faith, but to put those individuals in a local congregation.

It is interesting that in Philippi, Paul was compelled to choose a place of prayer as his first port of call, apparently because no synagogue was present as there was not the requisite number of males. Yet on his departure, he was able to leave behind a flourishing church.

Years later, some of those churches – the one in Ephesus for instance (along with six others) – received letters dictated to the Apostle John by the Lord Jesus Himself. The sheer weight of those messages attest to the importance Jesus places on His followers becoming part of a local congregation. The success of your Christian life is closely tied to the church of which you are a part.

THE EARLY CHURCH IN WORSHIP

Early Christians knew nothing of solitary religion. They gathered together frequently for worship, fellowship, and to break bread. The Scripture above is one of the earliest references to how the church met and worshipped. Believers in New Testament times met in the temple (daily), in the synagogues, and in homes. Their worship was marked by true devotion, with spiritual gifts such as tongues and prophecy in operation as we see in the first letter to the Corinthian church. They also had fellowship meals. The Apostles ministered the Word of God and led in prayer. Miracles of healing and deliverance were frequent occurrences and many came to faith daily. The people gave generously to meet the needs of the community. These were communities of love, giving, and service.

That is what the local church is. It is a community of people united by a shared faith in Jesus Christ as the Son of God and Saviour of the world. The community gathers to worship, to be trained in righteousness, to serve, and to demonstrate love for one another in different settings. They honour God together and work together to reach the world for Jesus. The Apostles were the undisputed leaders of the first Christians. They, as Paul often did, chose leaders within the local communities to head the local churches. Many of them were Jews and were accustomed to proceedings in the synagogues, but gradually, increasing numbers of Gentiles joined the church and assumed leadership.

The earliest surviving non-New Testament historical reference to the proceedings of a church service dates back to 150 AD, from a man known as Justin Martyr. Justin wrote a series of 'apologia' (defence of the faith), apparently, to explain Christian ways to the emperor. He sought to refute the gross misrepresentation of Christians so prevalent in the wider society of the time.

We learn in the first 'apologia' that the Christians met on the day called Sunday (which they called the Lord's day). Their gathering included: reading from Scripture (which he called the 'memoirs of the Apostles' and the 'prophets'), teaching and preaching by the presiding elder, prayers led by the presiding elder with the congregation joining in loud amens, and communion. Since Justin's purpose was to explain Christian ways to the emperor, I believe we are not expected to see his description as the norm or cast in stone.

Justo L Gonzalez, in 'The History of Christianity'[1] describes a typical second century communion service. It was in two parts. The first part included very lengthy Scripture readings, commentary, prayers and singing of hymns. The second was the communion service, with prayers and sharing of the communion elements. The entire proceedings lasted several hours.

There is no certainty that there was ever a time in the history of the church when everyone followed the same order and duration of service. The principal focus was on content. Church stereotypes engender huge frustration as worship styles invariably differ, and disappointment lurks for those who hold too rigidly to a form. Rather, we want to look at the content of the service. Is Jesus honoured and preached? Do the people there love God and one another?

There have always been difficult people in the church; even the Apostle Paul mentions a few of them. However,

---

1. Justo L Gonzalez, The History of Christianity, page 94

on the whole, you are struck by the sense of togetherness in the early church, the sense of community, of belonging one to the other. Other Christians are called brothers and sisters.

This must be the cry of the church today. We are not indifferent strangers sharing the same vessel to heaven; we are a team voyaging and working together for the same Master. Our lives are connected and intertwined. Christianity is anything but a solitary undertaking.

AURORA GOES TO 'CHURCH'

Aurora (not her real name) is a young convert. She has been a Christian for under five years. She came to the Lord in her home, knew nothing of church, and for a whole year she received spiritual nourishment through online Christian media. She watched hundreds of videos and knew a lot of 'doctrine'. Then she became involved with a group who would go together to visit churches from time to time, but refused to belong to any local church.

As she sought the Lord, she felt God pushing her to get involved in a local church and stop the roaming about. She visited a church she had been wanting to go to for a while, and stayed. Deep inside, she had known she was not meant to do this 'God thing' on her own.

Why? Was that an isolated experience or is local church belonging essential, when available, for the believer? Has the local church body become superfluous? Church services are available online and the world is awash with teaching, often free and easily accessible. This is in marked contrast to past centuries and in particular to the time of the early church. Most people then did not own personal copies of the Scriptures; it was read to them during congregational worship. Indeed, the first part of the celebration was devoted to Scripture reading and often lasted several hours.

I am not assuming that you are thinking these thoughts, but I have no doubt that someone is bound to voice them to you at some point. However, such thinking reflects a 'service to me' mindset. The believer is called to have a 'service to God' mindset.

> *We are not indifferent strangers sharing the same vessel to heaven; we are a team voyaging and working together for the same Master.*

Jesus established the church, validated the local church, and established gifts to be used by individuals in the context of the local church for the benefit of all. Every member is a part of this body and is described as having an important role to play in the wellbeing of the whole. If I only feed myself online, I forfeit the role that I am to play in the local community for the wellbeing of the brothers and sisters. Interaction is lost. Divine purpose is thwarted.

MY STORY

You may, like many today (including myself more than twenty years ago), already have many negative ideas about the church. You may feel some apprehension in joining a local congregation. You are not alone. Even after coming to faith in Christ – in the confines of my home – I was still very reluctant to mingle with believers. This was essentially because of deeply ingrained and quite irrational prejudices, albeit I thought differently at the time.

The thought of becoming part of an 'institution' was not wholly palatable, I cherished my freedom and balked at being compelled to attend church weekly. You may not feel so, in which case I heartily rejoice; you are wiser than many. However, many people labour under the weight of prejudices against all things that concern the church. When they come to Christ, they often would rather be a freelancer, sampling different religious offerings without committing to any local body. Distrust of church runs deep. 'Organised religion' is akin to a swear word.

Happily, our God is gracious, and shows mercy to the sceptical. In my case, a series of events led to my returning to church out of curiosity; somehow, He glued me in. I have never stopped 'doing' church since. I discovered those people were imperfect, but saved. It was the only opportunity to regularly gather to worship with people who loved God as I did. These people were different, but kindred.

You will find the same as you venture out to discover a local church with which to worship. That is what you should look for as you pray about a local church; look for people who genuinely love God, worship God, serve God, and love people. Churches vary in style, size, and focus but should be united around a fervent faith in Jesus, love for one another, and purity of life and conduct.

One other confession. We are not always wise. We love to be prescriptive. Barely saved, I was holding forth on the place of tongues in public worship (because I did not speak in tongues), on the minister's preaching style, etc. Avoid such foolishness. It will poison the sweet waters of your faith. Be like a baby: go, sing, drink milk, gurgle, grow, and enjoy yourself. Leave it to cantankerous believers to pontificate and fight over worship styles. You will do well to give such people a wide berth.

BENEFITS OF BEING PART OF A LOCAL CHURCH

When you join a community of believers meeting locally, you join a spiritual family. It is in this family that you will receive what you need to become mature spiritually. There, you will also have the opportunity to participate in Jesus' grand project of building the church. Let's break this down.

- You will be obeying Jesus.
- You will be taught the Scriptures.

- You will have the opportunity of worshipping God as a family member, not as a stranger peeping in; you will enjoy the blessing God pours out on His family gathered together.
- You will be encouraged by the works of God in the lives of other believers you know, rather than merely hear about them online.
- You will receive counsel in the affairs of life and help in navigating any uncharted waters of faith and culture.
- You will learn to pray, and you will have the privilege of praying on a regular basis with fellow believers. (More on this later.)
- You will receive support in the difficult seasons of life – spiritual, emotional and sometimes material.
- You will be trained to serve God, to share the gospel, to use your spiritual gifts and do whatever you are called to do.
- You will be trained in character through direct instruction, correction from leadership, or confrontation with the brethren.
- You will have the opportunity – on a weekly and daily basis – to be a blessing to the saints, in particular the new believers, the weak, and the vulnerable.
- You will have the privilege of participating in the

ministry of the local church and enhancing the role of Jesus' church in our generation.

As a postscript, only three of the New Testament letters were written to individuals. In the book of Revelation, the Lord sent letters through the Apostle John. All were written *to congregations* about the condition of those congregations. The only individuals mentioned were the troublemakers, the infamous Jezebel, for instance. Local congregations do matter to the Lord and should matter to every believer.

WHAT DO I DO?

So how do you go about finding a local church to join if you are not yet in one?

- The most natural thing, of course, would be to ask the person who brought you to the Lord, and go with them to church. Ask God to confirm that it is where you should be.

- If like myself you came to faith in Christ at home rather than in a church service, ask God to connect you with a local church family you can call your own. In my case, I did not have the good sense to ask because I had no intention of joining a church. God showed me mercy; He sent a friend to my house who invited me to her church. I went with her and ended up staying.

- Check the media for information on local churches.
- Ask your contacts – believers as well as non-believers. You would be surprised that even some non-believers would know about the churches in the area.
- Unless recommended by a person you trust, when possible, listen to the pastor's messages online and check out the website of the church before you go.

Don't rush off at the end of the service, and when they ask who is there for the first time, do stand up. Throw yourself right into it: go for midweek meetings, attend prayer meetings, or join a cell group. Remember, go, gurgle, and grow.

Based on an article I wrote a couple of years ago, this is my quick guide for a first-time visit to a church. It is written for mature Christians visiting another church, so it is written in a tongue-in-cheek manner. I do think it has pointers that will be of use to everyone. Enjoy.

First-time visit to another church – A quick guide

On any given Sunday, the world over, hundreds of thousands of churches open their doors for worship to members and visitors alike. In my many travels – from Africa to Asia, from Europe to Latin America to Oceania – I have, by Father God's infinite grace, visited churches aplenty. Big, small, boisterous, solemn, contemporary, traditional … there is an amazing diversity among God's people.

From that vantage point, you pick up a few pointers on what makes for an enjoyable church visit – for you and for the people you visit, especially if you are visiting as part of a church-hunting project. If you hope to one day join them, you might as well begin on the right foot.

As you read, don't worry if at times it seems as if I am reading your mail. No one told me about you, but you are not that unique; other people get the same things wrong. Here goes!

When you visit a new church

1. **Punctuality.** Do arrive on time. If you arrive when the service is already underway or halfway through the message, you will draw attention to yourself. It doesn't make you look important; it makes you look lazy and undisciplined.
2. **Respect.** Don't fight the ushers. If they ask you to sit somewhere, please do. Treat the church with as much respect as you would any secular place where there are sitting instructions. It is not your kingdom; it is God's, and no one is telling Him where to sit. Smile and obey.
3. **Attentiveness.** Try and get a good night's sleep before you come. You don't make a good impression by sleeping through the sermon the first time you show up. It will make it harder later to do your 'I'm

a prophet of God' number, not that we approve of course. But you get the gist.
4. **Decency.** Consider coming decently clothed. It is not legalism to expect not to have to contemplate another person's midriff, or exposed underwear as one lifts up holy hands to the Lord. Too tight, too low cut ... no; luckily, elegance does not require that. It is that 'je ne sais quoi' that you surely possess.
5. **Obedience.** Follow instructions. When the pastor says 'Let's stand', don't stay seated; you don't show anything but your own disagreeable nature when you do that. When they say it's time to be quiet, don't choose that opportunity to break out in song, because you feel 'led'. Those are spiritual guerrilla tactics, not becoming of you.
6. **Participation.** Get involved in the message, encourage the preacher, pray as you listen; don't sit back in silent defiance, daring them to teach you something you do not know. It shows that you neither respect nor love God's Word.
7. **Friendliness.** When the service is over, don't rush off as though you were fleeing the fires of hell; smile at someone, and thank the pastor for the service. Be relaxed and friendly; people don't usually bite in church ... not the first time you show up anyway.
8. **Humility.** When you introduce yourself, be humble, act like you are nobody. Understate your own

importance. In time, if they find out you are somebody (whatever that is), they will honour you. Conversely, treat them – particularly the pastor – with respect. Unless invited to, refrain from trying to prove you are his or her equal by placing yourself on a first-name basis. Christian brotherhood does not preclude civility. Showing respect will not condemn you to hell fire.

9. **Non-judgemental spirit.** If you do speak to the preacher, restrain every urge to pick holes in his or her sermon or argue a theological point to 'teach them something'. You have not been appointed as doctrine police and you are probably wrong anyway. Even if it means biting your tongue till it bleeds, refrain from running down their church, or criticising their worship – they were not singing to you. After all, it is God's business, isn't it? His alone.

10. **Generosity.** Finally, give an offering. Do not go to church empty-handed. You are a blessing, so bless. Some churches will say they do not expect first-timers to give. Give anyway.

There it is. Hopefully if you do all this, they will want you to come back. And more than anything else, you would have been a blessing to the Body of Christ and would not have strained anyone's nerves. They may even want you to join their church.

Some things in the article do not apply to you directly, and hopefully never will. Bear in mind that, as a believer, you are meant to honour other believers and the church of God.

*

Scriptures for meditation

Acts 2.42 – 'They devoted themselves to the apostles' teaching and to the fellowship, to the breaking of bread and to prayer.'

Colossians 3.16 – 'Let the word of Christ dwell in you richly as you teach and admonish one another with all wisdom, and as you sing psalms, hymns and spiritual songs, with gratitude in your hearts to God.'

Hebrews 10.24–25 – 'And let us consider how we may spur one another on towards love and good deeds. Let us not give up meeting together, as some are in the habit of doing, but let us encourage one another- and all the more as you see the Day approaching.'

Ephesians 4.11-12 – 'It was he who gave some to be apostles, some to be prophets, some to be evangelists, and some to be pastors and teachers, to prepare God's people for works of service, so that the body of Christ may be built up.'

I Peter 5.2-4 – 'Be shepherds of God's flock that is under your care, serving as overseers—not because you must, but because you are willing, as God wants you to be;...'

I Thessalonians 5.12-13 – 'Now we ask you, brothers, to respect those who work hard among you, who are over you in the Lord and who admonish you. Hold them in the highest regard in love because of their work. Live in peace with each other.'

[See also Romans 12.4-5; I Corinthians 12.14-16; Galatians 6.10]

*

Points to ponder

- When you join a community of believers meeting locally, you join a spiritual family. It is in this family that you will receive what you need to become mature spiritually.
- Church stereotypes engender huge frustration as worship styles invariably differ, and disappointment lurks for those who hold too rigidly to a form.
- You will have the privilege of participating in the ministry of the local church and enhancing the role of Jesus' church in our generation.

Discussion questions

1. Christianity is community. How true is this statement?
2. What are the benefits of being part of a local church?
3. Leaders are 'shepherds' whose role is to watch over you. How do you relate to them?
4. Community is service. How would you react to that?

Prayer

Father, thank You for my church.

I commit to be faithful. I ask you to teach, train and equip me for service. Give me rich and rewarding relationships. Make me a blessing to my church and to the kingdom. In Jesus' name. Amen.

3

Read

"The Bible is not an end in itself, but a means to bring men to an intimate and satisfying knowledge of God."

A. W. Tozer

(The Pursuit of God)

'...you must understand that no prophecy of Scripture came about by the prophet's own interpretation. For prophecy never had its origin in the will of man, but men spoke from God as they were carried along by the Holy Spirit' (2 Peter 1.20- 21).

The times are uncertain. A tyrant rules and fills the land with murder and venom. An old man finds himself in banishment, consigned to hard labour, a prisoner of conscience. And yet his will is not weakened, his resolve remains strong, his faith unwavering. He will see this through till the end.

Suddenly, he is overcome with the presence of God. His spiritual eyes open and wondrous things cascade before him. He sees Jesus. He hears a description of events the human mind labours to grasp. Visions flow before him, things unfathomable but for God; scenes of despair, terror, joy, celebration, from above and from beneath, a complex kaleidoscopic tapestry that generations to come will toil to decipher.

He has been chosen to carry a message, in the most unlikely context. The man, the Apostle John; the message, the last book of the Bible – the book of Revelation. He sees and he writes, and ends with the admonition that nothing be added to the words of this book – this book of revelation, but also prophetically, the bigger book of which Revelation will be but a final chapter: the Bible.

According to tradition, and as reported by such early fathers as Iraeneus, John suffered persecution at the hand of the emperor Domitian. He was sent into exile on the small Greek island of Patmos. While he was there, he received the stunning, divine visitations and visions that make up the Book of Revelation. At Domitian's overthrow, John's exile ended and he was able to return to live in Ephesus. There, he was a great comfort to the church, forever marked by the revelation received from the Lord. The book subsequently, though not without some opposition, became a part of the canon of Scripture.

What we witness in the final book of the Bible is truly exceptional. It is an instance of the process of divine inspiration of Scripture unfolding before our eyes. We get a glimpse into the communicating of the Word of God from God to man and from man to man.

Moses is the scribe God used to write the first five books of the Bible and he also described momentous events. However, we are not privileged to see the process by which he received the revelation of the events of creation, the fall, etc. It may well have been just as dramatic, or perhaps not in the least.

This brings us to the primary characteristic of the Holy Bible, something that you want to have in the forefront of your mind at all times. The Bible is the Word of God, inspired by God to be consigned into writing by human authors.

THE BIBLE MATTERS

God chose to use the seemingly indirect and unlikely means of the Bible to convey His heart and ways to us. It is an absolute treasure. In the Scriptures, you will hear God speak in direct form. You will see His ways reflected in His dealings with people. You will hear Jesus describe Himself and His mission. You will see examples of men and women who successfully walked with God and those who failed spectacularly and why. It is no wonder that the Apostle Peter said we have been given all that is requisite for life and godliness through the knowledge of God. It is all in there.

Structure

You may have heard that the Bible is a library, and it is. The Bible is a collection of sixty-six books. It is divided into the Old and New Testaments; it is made up of historical works, poetry, proverbs, letters, biographies, and meditations. These were written over more than 1,500 years through forty distinct human authors. The Old Testament is identical to the Jewish Scriptures. The New Testament opens with the events surrounding the births of John the Baptist and Jesus, and ends with the events of the end times. It covers the entire ministry of Jesus and His Apostles.

THE BENEFITS OF BIBLE READING, STUDY, AND MEDITATION

'All Scripture is God-breathed and is useful for teaching, rebuking, correcting and training in righteousness' (2 Timothy 3.16).

According to the above passage, God's Word is given by inspiration for a specific purpose. That purpose is not information; rather, it is instruction, rebuke, correction, conviction of sin, discipline, obedience, and holy living. It is for the purpose of Christ-likeness in thought, word, and deed. God uses His Word to teach and transform us, to make us like Jesus.

You see why it is imperative that you recognise the validity of the Bible. How can you submit to its teachings otherwise? You will treat them as good advice rather than mandatory lifestyles. The founding principle in approaching the Bible is recognising the superiority of God and His ways. 'Oh, God wants to change me?' Yes, He does. He takes us as we are and then He works to make us as He is. And it is wonderful. *The Bible…*

Gives understanding.

Have you ever thought about the fact that you can know nothing about God and His purpose for humanity without the Bible? There is some information about the historical Jesus outside the New Testament, but no revelation of His mission, person, and purpose. We tend to take that for granted, but it is a valid point. The Bible is our sole source of understanding of things spiritual.

Reveals God.

It reveals His nature, character, and design. As you read, seek to know the Lord. It is His book of self-revelation. It reveals God's love for us and draws us to become admirers and lovers of God. Read the Bible to encounter God not only to learn verses.

Reveals God's plan for humanity.

It reveals issues of redemption, intimacy, restoration. Everything we know about salvation, the new birth, holiness, and the end times comes from God's Word. It is there that we discover who man is, why he exists, and what his purpose is in Christ Jesus.

Reveals Jesus – as Saviour, Lord, and Friend.

Everything that can be known about Jesus is in the Bible. No other book reveals Him. The more time we spend meditating on the Bible with the help of the Holy Spirit, the more real Jesus becomes to us.

Instructs us in God's ways; first, by example:

> 'For everything that was written in the past was written to teach us, so that through endurance and the encouragement of the Scriptures we might have hope' (Romans 15.4).

God's Word is not a collection of pithy sayings or laws; it is a living book demonstrating the outworking of divine relationships with mankind. Life-and-blood characters fill its pages. Their examples of loyalty and faithfulness – and God's response to them – show us how to order our lives. We are encouraged by their stories. We are able to endure in adversity as we follow their examples. Counter examples are numerous as a deterrent to the wayward. To be forewarned, indeed.

Instructs us in God's ways; second, by precepts:

God's Word tells us what God wants, how to live in a 'manner worthy of the Lord'. It is the objective arbiter of good and evil, the moral compass by which we live. The New Testament letters tell us all the good that God has done for us in Jesus; they then promptly enjoin us to find out what pleases the Lord and to live in 'newness of life'.

God's Word is the only place where we find out what pleases the Lord. Once you come to Jesus, you are responsible for what you know or don't know. The French say 'nul n'est censé ignorer la loi', which translates roughly as 'none should be ignorant of the law'. Despite the huge body of legislation in France (the most extensive in Europe), all citizens are supposed to abide by them and know them. No breach can ever be justified on the grounds of ignorance. The psalmist cries out these words in Psalm 119.1-4:

> 'Blessed are they whose ways are blameless, who walk according to the law of the LORD. Blessed are they who keep his statutes and seek him with all their heart. They do nothing wrong; they walk in his ways. You have laid down precepts that are to be fully obeyed.'

Teaches us to obey and to live in holiness.

The new life in Christ is not one of permissiveness, but one of obedience. I fear this often gets lost in our cosy, sweet-gospel preaching aimed at avoiding giving offence to a generation that does not like to be told what to do. It's not about rules and regulations; it's about relationship. Perfectly true, yet relationships are governed by rules, otherwise they fall apart. We teach rules to our children all the time: respect for authority, obedience to teachers, to bosses, to the government, paying of taxes (or else). Despite our rebellious nature, we still recognise that we ought to do as we are told.

We agree that some forms of conduct are good for us and for the wellbeing of society, and that some are not. Often, the government decides such matters against our will and compels us to obey. How, then, can we possibly imagine that God does not have rules of proper behaviour that may be alien to us, sinners and rebellious creatures that we were? And He also requires us to obey; of course, it is for our own good, but it is also for the good of others. When God tells us to be generous, it is so we can be blessed, but it is also so the people we are supposed to show generosity to can be blessed.

When we disobey, we short-change ourselves and other people suffer. The epistles repeatedly draw a distinction between who we are now and who we used to be, what we do now and what we used to do. The gospel must affect our conduct. Faith, as James put it, without works is dead. I want to encourage you to choose a life of obedience. Listen to what Zechariah said about God's people; may it never be said of us:

> 'They made their hearts as hard as flint and would not listen to the law or to the words that the Lord Almighty had sent by his Spirit through the earlier prophets. So the LORD Almighty was very angry' (Zechariah 7.12).

Brings correction when we err.

The Word of God has, not only a preventive dimension, but also a corrective dimension. In writing to Timothy his spiritual son, the Apostle Paul wrote that 'all Scripture is God-breathed and is useful for teaching, rebuking, correcting and training in righteousness (2 Timothy 3.16). It is God's Word that shows us when and where we have gone astray. It prompts us to repentance. Thank God for the corrective ministry of God's Word or we would err consistently and remain indifferent until judgement falls. In Nehemiah chapter 8 we see the practical application of this point. The leaders of God's people gathered them together and Ezra the priest read the Word of God to them. They wept profusely. Why? Because they saw in the Word the error of their ways.

Teaches us how to deal with the devil.

The only one who thrives on your ignorance of God's Word is the devil. The Apostle Paul knew that and said 'we are not ignorant of his devices'. If you live in God's Word, you will not be ignorant. Evil is a present reality, and much of it is targeted at believers. Knowing God's Word puts you in a position where you can effectively resist the attacks of the evil one. We find out from God's Word how to keep the devil at bay.

Reveals the promises of God and our privileges in Christ.

Those are the 'these things' that Jesus spoke about when He said to seek first the kingdom and all these things shall be added unto you. It is from Scripture that you build a strong expectation of the goodness of God for your life. You are continually confronted with His goodness and His promises for you – spiritual, material, emotional, physical, etc. When you need His help, you will be happy to know He has already promised you help in the situation. You are not begging for something He is averse to doing. It makes a huge difference in your relationship with God.

Releases God's power.

As God's Word is absorbed, His power is released. God spoke, and all that exists came into being.

> 'By faith we understand that the universe was formed at God's command ...' (Heb. 11.3).

Jesus, when He was on the earth, would often speak a word and the power of God would perform what He spoke. He spoke and people were healed. He spoke and taught and they were edified. Many hung on to His every word. With His word, He stilled the waves.

> 'Then he got up and rebuked the winds and the waves, and it was completely calm' (Matt. 8.26).

With His word, He raised Lazarus from the dead. In the Old Testament, we are told that God watches over His Word to perform it. Today, as you meditate on God's Word, it is acting in your life. When you speak it, when it is preached, it contains the power to touch and change lives. So connect to the power!

Changes our mindset.

Last but not the least, God's Word helps us to change the way we think. Romans Chapter 12 calls it the renewal of the mind. Walking with God is not about grudgingly acquiescing to His demands. Rather, it is undergoing such transformation mentally that we come to agree with Him and we see the rightness of His ways. That is where God wants to bring you. So seek, not only to find things to obey, but also things to agree with. It is imperative that we agree with God. That means that we develop a biblical worldview rather than a worldview based on our society's current thinking.

HOW DO I READ THE BIBLE?

Simple. Open it up and read. True, yes, but perhaps a few pointers will help. Why? Many years ago, we would go out to the streets of Paris to talk to people. We would encourage them to read the Bible for themselves and not merely believe what the sceptics holding forth in the media trumpeted continually.

We found out, much to my surprise, that most people had little knowledge of the Bible. Few could distinguish between the Old and the New Testaments and many were put off by the size of the hefty book.

Can I tell you a secret? You can read the entire Bible comfortably within one week. I say comfortably, because the continuous reading time is 72 hours. I assume you will want to sleep and take breaks. Without thinking, we would tell people things like, 'Read the gospel of John' and we would be met with a puzzled, 'Whom? Where is that?' I realised I was assuming too much... I am going to pretend you have no Bible background whatsoever. That way we can be sure to leave no one scratching their heads. So how do you read?

First, remember the Bible is in two major parts, the Old and the New Testaments. The Old Testament deals with events leading from creation through the history of God's dealings with the people of Israel all the way to the last prophet. The New Testament takes off with the announcement of the birth of John the Baptist and the coming of Jesus. It ends with the events that will characterise the end of this age. Do not go rushing to the book of Revelation to find out in advance of the media what will happen at the end of the world. Let's talk about Jesus for now.

> *Walking with God is not about grudgingly acquiescing to His demands. Rather, it is undergoing such transformation mentally that we come to agree with Him and we see the rightness of His ways.*

Begin with Jesus

So where do you start reading? I suggest you begin with the New Testament, right at the beginning, with the accounts of the life and ministry of Jesus. The first person you need to know in the Scriptures is Jesus. Remember, He is the door, the way, the life. He is the One Person who cannot be circumvented. He is your passport to all things good and of God. So begin by gaining a healthy understanding of the Son of God. Know what He was like on the earth, what He did and said, and how He related to people. He is the perfect picture of God. He will answer your questions about what God is like!

Of course we will never know all that there is to know about God, otherwise He would cease to be infinite. Still, we can get a good head start here and now. Go from the gospels to the letters written to the early church. Take your time. Read them through several times. Then you can move on to the Old Testament. By then, I expect you will have acquired a better understanding of the connection and differences between the Old and the New. You will be in a better position to appreciate the amazing plan of God for humanity and for Israel presented in the Old Testament.

Do it daily, not as recreation

Read the Bible daily. Habits structure our lives and determine our future. Discipline is a good word for your spiritual life. Spiritual disciplines are the building blocks of your Christian life and the determinants of your success or failure as a spiritual disciple.

Read voraciously. It is God's Word; it deserves our attention. Many people approach their Bible reading as recreation, and their employment as serious. No. Bible reading and prayer are the most serious and most important activities you will engage in. In fact, much more so than your profession, your studies, or even church-related activity. Many rush to read a couple of verses in five minutes, then head off to work or school with an unrenewed mind to work for eight hours.

Do we work to the glory of God? Certainly. But if God is not glorified in me, He cannot be glorified through me. A person who is not inhabited by the Word of God cannot live to the glory of God despite paying lip service to the concept. Do not fall into that trap. Cut out some recreation and give more time to God's Word. Take holidays, unpaid if need be, and spend the time discovering God in His Word. He will reward your commitment.

Transformation, not information

Think about the Scriptures as your daily journey into God's heart. As you travel, you are changed. Your thinking is utterly and radically changed by God's Word. With that kind of perspective, it is obvious to see the value of daily reading. You will also avoid one bad habit that is sadly prevalent among believers, which is to employ Scripture as a tool to dissect others rather than to transform self. You know, don't you, that we are saved by grace, because of the great mercy of God? In ourselves, we did not measure up, but God took us as we were. He expects that, having received life and forgiveness, we would now let Him make us as we ought to be. His Word is one way He does that. The least we can do now is become students of the Word and allow God to make us over so that our lives can honour Him. That is transformation. The twelfth chapter of the letter to the church in Rome states it powerfully:

> "Therefore, I urge you, brothers, in view of God's mercies, to offer your bodies as living sacrifices, holy and pleasing to God– this is your spiritual act of worship. Do not conform any longer to the pattern of this world, but be transformed by the renewing of your mind. Then you will be able to test and approve what God's will – his good, pleasing, and perfect will"(Romans 12.1-2).

As you read, pray for understanding and transformation.

Chew on it

As you read, think over what you are reading. Mull it over, chew on it, run it through your mind, see the whys and wherefores, and let it settle in you. Also, in the course of your day, think about what you read. At work? Yes, at work. When you take a break, think about the morning's Scriptures and their implication for your life. Take a walk at lunchtime to meditate some more. Integrate the Word of God into your entire day. Some of the strangeness that people feel as Christians is because our lives are too compartmentalised: God thoughts at home and other thoughts elsewhere. We suffer from that dissonance.

Take notes

- Note the questions you have.
- Note the new things you are learning.
- Note the things you knew that struck you afresh. Some people call it journaling. You may use your computer, or you may prefer a handsome notebook. The choice is yours. When you reread your notes, you will be amazed at how much they will bless and encourage you. I have notebooks dating back very many years and I am always happy to peruse them afresh.
- Also note the scriptures that speak specially to your heart. Use a tablet, a phone, or index cards. Then take time to look through them again in the course of the day or the next day if you did your reading at night.

Listen

Technology has kicked in again to offer us another beautiful support for our Bible literacy: audio mp3s. I encourage you to get an audio Bible for your mp3 player and use it often. Use it at home, when commuting, and during your lunch break at work. Go to work listening to the gospel of John, for instance. Many of the biblical books are surprisingly short and quick to listen to. Let me give you an example to whet your appetite. It takes between two minutes and one hour to listen to the New Testament letters individually: 1.5 hours for the book of Revelation, 1.5 for the gospel of Mark; Luke and Matthew take 2.5 and John 2, while the book of Acts takes 2.25 hours. Not so daunting after all.

One other good way to listen is to follow along with your Bible. It helps focus and concentration immensely. It is also, in my view, extremely enjoyable. You have the choice of dramatised audio and straightforward reading. Never forget that the early church mostly listened to the Scriptures being read aloud to them. It is a very valid way of hearing the Word of God, but it should not be the only way.

Speak

Jesus said that we tend to say the things that are in our hearts. Well, He put it somewhat more forcefully than I just did. In Luke 6.45 He says that a good man brings good out of the good stored up in his heart and that the mouth speaks what the heart is full of. Unconsciously we do, but we can also do it consciously when we know that we have filled our hearts with good. I suggest you deliberately begin to speak God's Word. When you read or listen to the Scriptures, personalise them and vocalise them. It helps you see yourself in God's Word and to assimilate it to the point where it becomes part and parcel of your thinking. Then it will come out of your mouth in the different circumstances of life.

For instance, when you read that 'God made him who had no sin to be sin for us, so that in him we might become the righteousness of God ', it sounds good. But read this aloud: 'God made him who had no sin to be sin for me, so that in him I might become the righteousness of God.' Spoken out loud and personalised, it speaks to you very powerfully, doesn't it?

You can take the Scriptures that refer to what God has done for us in the new birth and apply this principle. The same goes for the general promises of God for His people. One of my favourite psalms, for instance, is Psalm 27. When I speak it out I am saying to myself, 'The Lord is my light and my salvation –whom shall I fear, the Lord is the stronghold of my life–, of whom shall I be afraid?" I am not just studying the fearlessness of the psalmist, I am also affirming my own fearlessness and confidence in God. The outcome is that the Word builds faith in me. I am encouraged to tackle head on the challenges of life because I am assured of God's protection even in the midst of difficulty. And that is only the beginning of the psalm. Read through it and you will find what an utter delight it is.

As you progress in your spiritual life, you will also learn to study specific topics in-depth. There are many tools available for that: Bible software, the internet, good books, and concordances. However, I would recommend that you keep it simple. Make the reading of the Scriptures your primary focus. In your local church you will have people come alongside you to assist you. Thank God for His Word every time you read it. What a privilege to have access to God's Word as easily as we do. Past generations did not always enjoy this privilege in the same measure.

A MICRO DOSE OF BIBLE HISTORY

The Old Testament is the Jewish Scriptures. They already existed as canon in their current form at the time of Jesus. The greatest testimony we have to their inspiration is the attitude of Jesus towards the Old Testament. He quoted it extensively and considered it to be the Word of God, and Himself as its fulfilment. The New Testament books were written in the first century. We do not have the exact dates since we do not have the original texts. However, the very early date of many of the manuscripts found so far certainly confirms that they were written very early.

The gospels were written to tell the accounts of the life of Jesus. Three of them are very similar, and they are called the synoptic gospels – Matthew, Mark and Luke. Mark is considered to have served as a scribe for Peter. Luke was the medical man who accompanied the Apostle Paul on his missionary journeys. He endeavoured to compile a well-researched and orderly account of the life of Jesus. The gospel of John was written from a slightly different perspective by the then elderly John. These were contemporaries of Jesus. The book of Acts recounts the early missionary endeavours of the church, in particular of the Apostle Paul. The letters of the Apostles were circulated among the churches and widely copied. They were used by early believers along with the Old Testament Scriptures. The book of Revelation narrates visions of Christ and His end-time kingdom, as given to the Apostle John.

Early letters of some church fathers quoted the books and confirm their general usage and acceptance as authoritative Scriptures from an early date. The discovery of very ancient manuscripts in Egypt confirms the rapid spread of the church from Palestine to Europe, Asia, and Africa. The Scriptures were copied and then translated. Many manuscripts exist in Syriac, Coptic, Ethiopic, Armenian, etc. We get a glimpse of their early use in worship from chapter 67 of Justin Martyr's (100-165) *First Apology*. It reads:

> 'And on the day called Sunday, all who live in cities or in the country gather together to one place, and the memoirs of the Apostles or the writings of the prophets are read, as long as time permits; then, when the reader has ceased, the president verbally instructs, and exhorts to the imitation of these good things'.

Another interesting piece of history is the Muratorian canon or fragment. It is a copy of a late 2nd century document containing the earliest known list of New Testament books. It includes twenty-two of the twenty-seven books of the New Testament. Athanasius, one of the 4th century fathers of the church, was famous as a staunch defender of the doctrine of the divinity of Christ. He was also known for circulating the first list of New Testament Scriptures that is identical to the New Testament as it stands today.

Inevitably, as is to be expected with humans, certain individuals began early on to produce spurious writings and strange doctrines. Prominent among these were the Gnostics. The Apostle John himself, history tells us, had to deal with some such individuals. The story is told that he once fled a bath-house without bathing on seeing a certain Cerinthius inside. *'Let us fly, lest even the bath-house fall down, because Cerinthus, the enemy of the truth, is within'*[1], he cried as he left. The Apostle Paul enjoined in his letters that warnings be given to those who would teach strange doctrines. Jesus, writing to the seven churches in the opening chapters of the book of Revelation, rebuked some for following strange doctrines.

Another famous purveyor of strange doctrines was Marcion (2nd century). He considered that Jehovah, the God of the Old Testament, was different from the God and Father of Jesus, who would be the God of the New Testament. He produced his own list of 'authoritative' Scriptures, which included the epistles of Paul and the gospel of Luke shod of all references to Judaism. He set up his own church, consecrated bishops, and led many astray. It was he

---

1. Against Heresies (Book III, Chapter 3). Iranaeus. Ante-Nicene Fathers, Vol. 1.

who Polycarp, a disciple of the Apostle John, is said to have addressed as the firstborn of Satan.

In time the church saw the wisdom of giving official recognition to the Scriptures considered authoritative by the church at large to protect believers from charlatans and heretics, and to permit the translation of the Scriptures for missions purposes. They were required to bear the mark of apostolic approval. A synod was convened in AD 393 in Hippo that gave the oficial list of all 27 New Testament books, further confirmed later in AD 397 at the synod of Carthage. The books of Scripture were thus universally recognised by the Church. The hand of God was manifest in this extraordinary concord. It was an acknowledgement of what the Holy Spirit had already established in the practice of the churches. No book was recognised that was newly written or without prior acceptance and use by the church.

God was pleased to use humans and even the vagaries of their existence to communicate His truth and reveal His heart. By the witness of His Spirit these texts came to be used and accepted in His church. By the power of His Spirit, events were orchestrated to bring a unity of purpose and an agreement on that which He had established.

Treat it as precious.

We now have God's Word available to us. Most people in the world have access to it in their own language. We can both read and listen to it. It is an immense privilege.

I encourage you to never lose your sense of gratitude that God has taken so much trouble to communicate His heart to us.

> 'Do not let this Book of the Law depart from your mouth; meditate on it day and night, so that you may be careful to do everything written in it. Then you will be prosperous, and successful' (Joshua 1.8).

A MICRO DOSE OF APOLOGETICS

The Bible is the primary revelation of Jesus. There are snippets of history that confirm the biblical picture of Him; no other source can flesh out His Person as the Bible does.

Faith in Jesus has to be faith in the Bible that reveals Jesus. There are many who pooh-pooh the Bible, but claim to love Jesus ... conveniently forgetting that they only know Him by the very book they decry. Surely, the proof of the pudding is in the eating. Everything we have seen so far will certainly prove that God's Word is true and works in our lives today. That certainly was the case for me; God convinced me to believe His Word. However, people are asking valid questions. Perhaps you are, too, and one way of helping them inch nearer to Jesus is to answer their questions.

Let us look at issues of inspiration, consistency, accuracy, and authenticity.

Divine inspiration

In the second letter to Timothy, we read the following:

> 'All Scripture is God-breathed and useful for teaching, rebuking, correcting and training in righteousness' (2 Timothy 3.16).

This means that you have in your possession a book of infinite value. You have a book that echoes with the very voice of God. The voice of God can be heard in these varied sixty-six books that form a composite whole. Despite the distance in time between composition periods of the books (Moses wrote circa 1400 BC and John 95 AD), the harmony, the message, and the perspective shock by their unity. It is a miracle that many today are oblivious to. The Scriptures are also remarkable in that God used these human authors, sometimes without them even being conscious that they were composing Scripture. God used improbable situations, situations of difficulty, to bring out His Word in an unexpected way.

No life situation is a hindrance to being used by God. Think of John exiled on Patmos, or Paul imprisoned in Caesarea and then in Rome. Abraham's childbearing issues became a powerful prophecy of the Messiah. It is imperative that you understand the inspiration of the Scriptures and receive the Bible as God speaking to you, not Paul, not Peter, though we tend to use their names. If you will ask Him, He will show you His presence through His Word.

God has taken the trouble to communicate this priceless book to us. It stands to reason that He will confirm fully in our hearts that the Bible truly is His and can be believed. We are spirit beings made for communication with the divine Being and He will attest in our hearts that this is truly His Word.

I am aware that many are, like I was, extremely sceptical of the contents of the Bible. Even though I came to faith in Christ reading the New Testament, I still had deep misgivings about the Bible as a whole. I was fearful of finding something in it that would shake my faith; a rather irrational perspective, granted, but there it was. It was the result of years of brainwashing against the Bible and of the Bible-bashing I myself indulged in with glee before my conversion. God was gracious to submerge me in revelation and woo my recalcitrant mind over to Himself.

Ultimately, it is through the Holy Spirit that we receive firm conviction that the Bible is divinely inspired. If you wonder at the inspiration of Scripture, I invite you to pray and ask God to show you. One positive step is that you believe it enough to have received salvation through the preaching of the Bible. It is God's testament for you.

Consistency and accuracy

Bear in mind while reading the Bible that it is one consistent narrative. No one ever told me that during my early Christian walk and I often wondered at all the different stories and sub-stories and seemingly irrelevant events. It was one big mystery book. In fact, one single thread connects all these plots and subplots, running from creation through redemption all the way to the end of the times. It is the story of redemption. We see Creation, the Fall, the promise and preparation for redemption, the act of redemption, and the prophecy of renewal. It is the story of God's gracious dealings with man – past, present and future. Every story, theme, and subtheme is connected to this major narrative.

As you read the Bible, you will see this picture much more clearly than I can describe it to you here. You will find yourself better able to understand those passages commonly referred to as the difficult passages or those problematic Old Testament passages that involve violence and antisocial behaviour. The Old Testament tells the story of the preparation of a people for the coming of the Saviour who would usher in a new era, a new way of relating to God and to our fellow humans. It is a wonder to see this diverse collection of books with such internal harmony of message and perspective. This is not the work of one lone individual foisting his hallucinations on us as the revelation of God. It is coherent, consistent, inspired, and accurate.

One more salient feature of the Bible that you will do well to embrace is its accuracy. Scripture is accurate historically, prophetically, and doctrinally. You will notice how specific the Bible is about times, places, people, etc. It thereby opens itself up to charges of falsehood in the event of those things being contradicted by extrabiblical sources. By and large, when outside documentation exists, the biblical narration of history has been borne out. It is prophetically accurate. Scholars estimate that about 300 prophecies in the Old Testament have found their fulfilment in the New. It is doctrinally accurate; indeed, the Old Testament is affirmed by Jesus Himself.

Accuracy also means that the content of the text, the New Testament in particular, reflects the events that actually took place. These ancient narratives were not embellished legends. The New Testament came to us from eyewitnesses or those who walked with eyewitnesses and apostles, such as Luke. They were contemporaries of Jesus. It is more than likely, as some scholars believe, that Matthew – a tax collector and an educated man – took notes as Jesus taught. Indeed, it was customary for disciples of rabbis to take notes of what their leader said and did. Come to think of it, it would have been strange for them not to have done so. Manuscript evidence shows that the texts were written very soon after the death of Jesus, and not hundreds of years after, as some have erroneously claimed.

Did the miracles actually happen? Yes. Do miracles still happen today? Yes. Many respected Western apologists would even explain away the supernatural elements of Scripture in a bid to deflect the scorn of liberals and atheists. Even some sections of the Church believe that God has retired from the performance of works of wonder, but some of us respectfully disagree. The supernatural dimension of Scripture was neither a mistake nor merely a way of communicating with ancient peoples with a primitive mindset. The supernatural still exists today. Some of us have first hand experience of miracles, divine healing, and of dealing wih persons affected by demonic activity. We rather marvel at the arrogance of persons who are ignorant of such basic dimensions of the human experience. The Holy Spirit is still confirming the Scriptures today by performing miracles through His church.

> *Ultimately, it is through the Holy Spirit that we receive firm conviction that the Bible is divinely inspired.*

God works with people today, and His power has not changed. In the same way that Jesus made Himself totally available to the Father for ministry on the earth, we ought to make ourselves totally available. It is more the lack of available and willing people that hinders the working of miracles than the unwillingness of God or untruthfulness of the Scriptures. Believe in the supernatural; it is perfectly natural for people who serve a supernatural God.

Authenticity

Another point you have to settle is the fact that the Bible in your hand is the same as when it was inspired by God. Why is that important? Because, in our day, charges of distortion are levelled at the Bible. The original texts were inspired and accurate, but maybe the ones we have today have been corrupted. What if the Church conspired to change them? At some point in your Christian walk, you will likely encounter these questions or some other variant of the same sentiments.

Not having grown up in the Western world, I was not accustomed to that particular mode of attack on the Bible. In my world, you either believed it was inspired or you did not. I did not. I believed the whole "Christianity thing" was the white man's tool to enslave us. (Yes, I did think that for a season.) When I came to know the Lord, my concern was mostly about the inspiration and accuracy of the Scriptures, and perhaps the palatability of it. As I had strong views about everything, I feared I would happen upon things I simply could not agree with.

It seemed perfectly natural that if God did inspire the Scriptures at some point, He would have taken pains to preserve them. Surely preserving them required much less sagacity and skill than communicating them to mere mortals to begin with, right? He spoke through the centuries, through very diverse persons. He deployed considerable effort dealing with the vagaries of human nature and making do with the extreme primitiveness of human means of notation and conservation. Would He, when it was all done, simply let it all go to waste? Would He stand by and watch it being destroyed and corrupted without batting an eyelid?

I think not. To affirm that the original Scriptures were inspired, but our current ones are corrupted, is illogical. It is, in a sense, a rubbishing of the God who inspired them. Even if my peculiar argument does not hold with you, you can still trust your current text of the Bible because documentary evidence abounds as to its authenticity.

Let me share with you some of the insights from respected scholars on the matter of authenticity. The New Testament is known to be the single most credible ancient text in existence. Why? Because of the overwhelmingly large body of manuscripts available in the original Greek as well as in Latin and other languages. There are more than 5,600 Greek manuscripts of the New Testament.

Apologists offer a striking comparison between the wealth of documentary evidence for the New Testament and the paucity of evidence for the revered Greek classical writings. Compared to the more than 5,600 Greek manuscripts of the New Testament, Homer's *Iliad*, on the other hand, has but a scant 643 copies, the *Annals* of Tacitus, 20 copies, Caesar's *Gallic wars*, 10 copies [2]. There are a further 10,000 Latin manuscripts and thousands more Syriac,

---

2. Josh McDowell 'New Evidence that demands a verdict', page 38.

Coptic, Armenian, Ethiopic and other versions of the New Testament. The textual variants in these manuscripts have no impact on the message of Scripture and the essential doctrines of the faith.

The oldest surviving portion of the New Testament is the John Ryland papyrus. It is dated in the early part of the second century, less than fifty years after the date of composition. The most ancient New Testament manuscripts from the first 300 years after composition contain collectively the entire New Testament many times over. In contrast, other ancient works have zero copies that date back to the first 300 years. In fact the oldest copies of Tacitus's *Annals, Caesar's Gallic Wars* and the complete manuscripts (20 in all) of Livy's *History of Rome* are over 1000 years after composition[3]. And yet Western civilization very comfortably embraces these classical works as authentic while deriding the Scriptures. A question of bias?

Sometimes nonbelievers or proponents of religions that hold to a unilingual religious book complain about the many translations of the Bible, claiming they have distorted the text. Not so. The translations are based on very reliable manuscripts. From the beginning, Christianity was a religion of translation. The focus was on making God's Word available to people in their language, which explains the very early date of some Latin, Syriac and Coptic manu-

---

3. Wilder Terry, Cowan Steven, *In Defense of the Bible*

scripts. Interestingly, the world of Jesus was a multilingual world of Aramaic, Latin and Greek.

Many complain about the inevitable loss in meaning when a text is translated, traduttori traditori ("translators traitors"). Yet even for people who do not know the original languages, a comparison of different versions is quite adequate in seeing where nuances lie, if any. Furthermore, as a professional translator and interpreter, I navigate through and compare various translations of the Scriptures in each of four even five languages. I marvel at the integrity of God's Word and the extent to which meaning has been preserved and remains concordant from French to English, to Spanish, to Portugese. I also celebrate all those men and women who have devoted their lives to translating God's Word.

An extra bonus is that the writings of the early Fathers contain all of the New Testament as we have it today, save a handful of verses. They used the same Bible and honoured it as God's Word. Who are we, several centuries later, to purport to know more than they did about the content of these Scriptures? But humility has never been the forte of modern man.

One day, as I conversed with some friends, one of them arrogantly asserted that the Dead Sea Scrolls had proved the Old Testament to be patently false. They could not have been further from the truth. When those goatherds happened upon the cave and discovered the manuscripts, they had no idea what impact they would have on the world. Among those scrolls is the book of Isaiah, one thousand years older than the oldest existing manuscript of the Hebrew Old Testament. Indeed, the existing Hebrew texts of the Old Testament are quite far apart in date from the time of writing.

The earliest Old Testament scriptures are paradoxically the Septuagint, the Greek translation of the Old Testament. So the discovery of these ancient scrolls was quite an event. Rather than invalidating the later manuscripts, the Isaiah scroll was a resounding confirmation of the integrity of those texts. A thousand years had introduced no more than cosmetic changes to the text. According to one scholar, they are identical up to 95 percent, and the remaining variants are of a non-substantive nature. Today, in our era of photocopying and printing, we may fail to appreciate the extraordinary nature of this find; it testifies to the fact that God had watched over His Word and preserved it.

I hope that by now you are marvelling at the great sagacity of our God. God, in His wisdom, equipped His people with the capacity to faithfully copy texts by hand. Some of the scribes would literally count every word to ensure nothing had been left out. It appears that they would, after copying, bury the older manuscript in a clay jar. This would explain the relative paucity of more ancient Old Testament texts. In their day, new was better, you see. The Christians, perhaps because of Gentile influence, tended to keep the older manuscripts and not destroy them. Christians can be assured of the reliability of the texts in their hands.

God is still speaking.

The Bible is God speaking to us. It is remarkably reliable, authentic, and accurate. It is God's instrument for divine revelation, life transformation and spiritual maturity. He speaks through it today as He has always done. So let it become an integral part of your life. Hold it dear, treat it as precious. It will yield its fruit in your life and fill it with grace, peace and victory.

*

Scriptures for meditation

2 Timothy 3.16 – 'All Scripture is God-breathed and useful for teaching, rebuking, correcting, and training in righteousness.'

Hebrews 4.12 – 'For the word of God is living and active. Sharper than any double-edged sword, it penetrates even to dividing soul and spirit, joints and marrow; it judges the thoughts and attitudes of the heart.'

1 Corinthians 2.13 – 'This is what we speak, not in words taught us by human wisdom but in words taught by the Spirit, expressing spiritual truths in spiritual words.'

Jeremiah 15.16 – 'When your words came, I ate them; they were my joy and my heart's delight, for I bear your name, O LORD, God Almighty.'

Isaiah 55.11 – 'So is my word that goes out from my mouth: It will not return to me empty, but will accomplish what I desire, and achieve the purpose for which I sent it.'

Romans 10.17 – 'Consequently faith comes from hearing the message, and the message is heard through the word of Christ.'

Matthew 4.4 – 'Jesus answered, "It is written: "'Man does not live on bread alone, but on every word that comes from the mouth of God.'"

[See also Matthew 24.35; Psalm 119.9; Isaiah 66.2]

*

Points to ponder

- God was pleased to use humans and even the vagaries of their existence to communicate His truth and reveal His heart.
- There is some information about the historical Jesus outside the New Testament, but no revelation of His mission, person, and purpose.
- It takes between two minutes and one hour to listen to the New Testament letters individually.

Discussion questions

1. The Bible is for transformation, not information. Comment.
2. What does it mean that the Bible is 'God-breathed'?
3. List five benefits of Bible reading, meditation and study.
4. Give a few pointers on how to read the Bible.

Prayer

Father, thank You for giving me Your Word.

I commit to becoming a lifelong student of the Word. Thank You for the Holy Spirit who leads me into all truth. Transform me with Your Word Lord and use me to communicate Your truth to my generation. In Jesus' name. Amen

4

Pray

'Then Jesus told his disciples a parable to show them that they should always pray and not give up' (Luke 18.1).

Every evening, the girls would troop into the chapel. It seems to me that there was a Mass said daily. There was singing, and prayers were offered. We dutifully said amen. I do not remember minding very much. We would kneel and mumble our prayers. I do not remember anyone in the congregation ever praying out loud. The priest, Father McKenna, did. He was from Ireland, as were the Reverend Sisters. We thought him young and handsome. We often wondered for what earthly reason he would leave his native Ireland to live a celibate life in Nigeria. Why spend his life saying Mass to young girls and boys (from the neighbouring boy's school) who had anything but God on their minds? We dreamt up romantic entanglements between him and the Reverend Sisters. After all, holed up in that convent, anything could happen.

One prayer exercise we found as discomfiting as it was moving and enchanting, was the Stations of the Cross. If the intent was to give us a picture of the sufferings of Jesus, it was extremely effective. Many times, with the prolonged kneeling and the lure of sleep, my suffering was so acute I thought I was close to death myself. But I liked the singing, I had my special seat, and I could recite the three Masses Father McKenna said by heart. Prayer was a fairly quiet affair. You did not speak too loudly to God.

Then everything changed. One of my seniors, a friend of my sister's, became very religious. She had been something of a hell raiser, but then she changed into a nice, gentle soul. She began to give me things to read, forbidden tracts from overseas. The Sisters were totally against such strange reading. They had odd titles like 'You Must Be Born Again'. They talked about the end of the world, things that fired the imagination of the young teenager that I was. I must have said a prayer to receive Jesus, not that I knew what that meant, but she began to take me with her to pray. The school had massive outside bathrooms that were empty during the day and off we would go to pray. She would kneel in one and I in another and she would pray in this language she called tongues – very deeply, very intensely, and very sincerely. I was not to be outdone, I pretended I also spoke this language and would pray twisting my tongue and making funny noises.

I longed to speak it, so I faked it, hoping it would happen. Yes, I did, and lived to tell the tale; how astounding the mercies of God. I followed along with this until she left school. I think I simply enjoyed the bizarreness of the whole thing, and those tracts were captivating. But she would pray, out loud in tongues, for long. That kind of praying was new to me. Prayer for her was serious business. It fired my imagination, but, as they say in the American South, I had not got religion. Not yet.

After she left, and I was left to my own devices, I wandered back into the pen of the unrighteous. But I had seen another form of prayer and I would never forget it. God, apparently had not forgotten me either. Today I love to pray. I no longer twist my tongue to make funny sounds, but I love to lead people in prayer. Today I write tracts, but not about the end times. God communicates with us in His Word and we communicate with Him in prayer.

Prayer is a gift I will encourage you to embrace. Prayer takes different forms. When we come to know the Lord, we are often influenced in our outward expression of prayer by our church environment or even our culture. In this chapter, I will touch on some fundamentals of prayer that will help you to begin to love praying. They will enable you to gain freedom from impediments to prayer – spiritual, cultural, etc. – and become a mighty man or woman of prayer.

Set that as your goal: to become mighty in prayer. You can, you should, you must, and dare I say, you will.

THE GIFT OF PRAYER

Prayer is a gift? Yes, it is. Prayer is the opportunity given mortal man to approach, talk to, and hear the immortal, invisible, holy God. It is an unquantifiable privilege to have the ear of God. That God would listen to what you say, pay attention to it, and respond is a wonder you would want to take time to think about.

If anyone had the right to ignore you, it would be God. If anyone had occupation enough to consider you irrelevant, it would be God. If anyone had better and worthier creatures to devote time and attention to, it would be God. Yet to love and to pray as we ought, we must understand how much of a gift prayer is. It is a thrill to wake up in the morning and know that the whole world may not stand still at your rising; your neighbours may not notice your awakening; your entourage may resent the disruptiveness of your presence; but the Lord Most High awaits your conversation and your company. You marvel and exclaim with the psalmist, 'What is man that you are mindful of Him?'

We must be creatures of wonder in the presence of a merciful and gracious God. I do not deny that many a time we have had occasion to wonder if indeed He noticed or heard us, but we were in ignorance. His Word, His primary means of communication with us, makes it abundantly clear that God listens and hears. Think about it for a few minutes; when you speak, the Most High God listens to you intently and hears everything you say. And He responds.

The good news is that you can pray. Anyone can pray. Prayer is accessible; prayer is possible. We were originally wired to communicate with God so it is already part of our makeup. The wires may need to be detangled and reconnected, but God is able to do all that and more. Anyone with a mind and a mouth can pray. It is simply talking to God. When people say they cannot pray, they are not thinking of mumbling to God as I did those many years ago in the chapel. They are thinking of the 'powerful', vocal praying they hear other Christians pray or the long hours that some people put into prayer.

Many years ago I counselled a couple who had just come to Christ, and I encouraged them to begin to pray together. The man was very reluctant to pray with his wife, as she was very eloquent in prayer and he could barely speak. He felt inadequate, and it seemed as if prayer was just not his thing. Shortly after, as he grew spiritually – receiving prayer and attending prayer meetings regularly – he lost his initial inhibitions and became very active, very vocal in prayer.

Everyone can pray. You can pray. But why must you pray?

WHY PRAY?

Why on earth *not* pray? We pray because it is a privilege to communicate with God and we have been given the honour of fellowshipping with Him.

We also pray because God commands us to pray. It is not a suggestion, but a clearcut instruction from God's Word. We are told to *'Pray continually' (1 Thessalonians 5.17).* Jesus Himself had a very vibrant prayer life, so much so that His disciples pleaded with Him to teach them to pray. And on several occasions He gave instructions on how to pray. Quite obviously, we are expected to pray. Prayer is obedience to Christ, and prayerlessness is disobedience. *Colossians 4.2 says, 'Devote yourselves to prayer, being watchful and thankful'.* It is not a recreational activity, something we do for relaxation or if we have time on our hands. It is one of the two most important things we can do with our time. God requires us to pray.

> 'I want men everywhere to lift up holy hands in prayer, without anger or disputing' (1 Timothy 2.8).

We are required to pray because we have need of the fruits of prayer – the fruit of intimacy, love shared with God; the fruit of revelation of truth; the fruit of character transformation and holiness; the fruit of freedom from demonic bondage and breakthrough in our lives. We are instructed to pray because we sorely need to pray. For God to move on our behalf, prayer must be made. For us to know God's purpose and direction for our lives – and to follow that purpose accurately – prayer must be made. Every good plan of God for us must emerge from the womb of prayer. We pray to release God's power into our circumstances and the circumstances around us.

> *We pray because God has work to do that can only be done through prayer. Prayer is more than fellowship and self-maintenance. It is about winning victories for God, conquering opposition, destroying adversity, and bringing to bear the will of*

God in a particular situation. It is about partnering with God to set people free of affliction, to bring healing and deliverance. It is about influencing the course of history in line with the will of God. God requires His people to pray because it is His invitation into the earth to change things.

How many things that God desires to do on earth are hindered because His people fail to pray? We can have the privilege of being God's agents to save people from untimely death or other disasters when we pray. We pray because it is commanded of us, because it is a privilege to pray, and because it is highly beneficial to us personally and to other people. Happy are those who live in the company of praying men and women, happy are those who are praying men and women.

If prayer is this useful, how then should one pray? And can everyone pray this kind of lifesaving prayer?

HOW DO I PRAY?

Several centuries ago, the disciples of Jesus had exactly the same question, so they went to Jesus and said, 'Lord, teach us to pray.' Jesus obliged and taught them to pray.

Many years ago, I decided to emulate them and began to pray, '*Lord, teach me to pray.*' And I believe the Lord obliged and taught me while also enabling me to help other people to pray. I encourage you, pray this prayer continually: 'Lord, teach me to pray.'

A couple of pointers

Several years ago when we started our television programme, I filmed a series of four messages on prayer based on a message I had preached in the church. It ranks high in popularity among all the series we have done and I think that it is because of the simplicity of the approach presented.

The Lord had laid on my heart to encourage His people to pray by giving them two basic principles – availability and regularity. You can develop a strong prayer life, even as you grow in knowledge and understanding of proper doctrine ... you can, if you will make yourself available, if you will give God the time He requires. Too often we mumble quick prayers and dash off to do the 'important' things in life. Then on Sundays we come to worship God and try to 'smooth His ruffled feathers' by lying through our teeth that He is everything to us. We continue to struggle with finding time to pray. Time is not our problem; it is a change of attitude that we need. We find time to chat on the phone and to keep up with the antics of our favourite sitcom characters. Make yourself available to pray and you will not regret it.

The second thing is regularity. Pray regularly. You have heard that your habits determine your success in life. Prayer is a habit that will make you. It will make you mighty; it will make you strong; it will make you close to God; it will make you a satisfied Christian. Forge the habit of regular prayer. Set time aside every day, preferably the same time, so you never even have to think about it. Don't worry about the technicalities of prayer. Simply be available, be regular, and trust that the Holy Spirit will do the rest.

Say thank you

Begin by saying thank you. Gratitude never fails. The Word of God enjoins us consistently to thank God for all His goodness. His goodness is boundless, eternal, and undeserved. Our gratitude should be unceasing, forever, and humble. Almost 200 times in the Scriptures, and over forty times in the epistles of Paul, we are called to give thanks. Listen to Jeremiah's words:

> 'Give thanks to the LORD Almighty, for the LORD is good; his love endures forever' (Jeremiah 33.11).

- Thank Him for saving you.
- Thank Him for Jesus, for the cross, and for the resurrection.
- Thank Him for opening your eyes to see the beauty of Christ
- Thank Him for the Holy Spirit.
- Thank Him for all that you are and all that you have (well, the good bits).

If you can say thank you, you can pray. If you don't feel inspired, make a list. By the time you get to the end of your list, you will probably be in tears as you contemplate the goodness of God. It's a good habit to acquire, writing down the good works of God on your behalf.

Praise and adore Him

Add praise to your 'thank you'. Bless Him for His greatness and His works. Express your admiration. Do it with vigour and vitality; do it with conviction. Read the following psalm, Psalm 150 (HCSB); look how vibrant and exuberant it is:

Praise the Lord

Hallelujah!
Praise God in His sanctuary.
Praise Him in His mighty heavens.
Praise Him for His powerful acts;
praise Him for His abundant greatness.

Praise Him with trumpet blast;
praise Him with harp and lyre.
Praise Him with tambourine and dance;
praise Him with flute and strings.
Praise Him with resounding cymbals;
praise Him with clashing cymbals.

Let everything that breathes praise the Lord.
Hallelujah!

Amazingly, you can feel the energy and joy of the psalmist's words. You can hear the trumpet; you are almost covering your ears at the sound of the cymbals resounding and clashing. The 'hallelujah' at the end sounds like thunder. Praise Him exuberantly. That is the testimony of Scripture.

Then adore Him. When we begin to thank God and praise Him for His goodness to us, our hearts grow tender towards Him. To adore Him is to recognise His majesty and to worship Him in humility. To adore Him is to switch to pouring your love out on Him and telling Him not just how great His works are, but how utterly beautiful He is. One of the loveliest acts of the human heart is to pour love and adoration out to God. Jesus becomes extremely precious to us and we want nothing more than to sit with Him because we love being with Him. We seek nothing more than to honour Him. 'He is altogether lovely,' as the Scriptures say (Song of Solomon 5.16).

> *Companionship with God is addictive. I can desire for you no other addiction. Be addicted to the presence of God.*

We were made to love, we were made to bow, and we were made to be struck with admiration for God. We were made to fall prostrate before His majesty. You can thank God, you can praise God, you can love God ... you can pray.

Pray the Scriptures

The chapter on the Word of God explains the need to speak the Scriptures and appropriate them for oneself. You declare like the psalmist, *'the Lord is my light and my salvation, I will fear no one. The Lord is the stronghold of my life, I am utterly fearless. When evil people gather to attack me in any way, shape or form, they stumble, fall and fail completely...'* and so on and so forth (Psalm 27.1-2). You get the gist. That is praying. It is confessing God's Word, saying what God says in His Word.

Make a habit of praying the Word of God. Use it for thanking God. Use it for praising and worshipping. Use it for declaring the promises of God in your life. Use it for presenting your requests to God.

Present requests

Prayer is agreeing with God to ask Him to do what He has promised to do. Let me share two prayer secrets with you. The first is to pray according to divine priorities. Jesus taught us about divine priorities in the prayer form we call the Lord's Prayer. When you read through this prayer in Matthew chapter 6, you will find that the first three requests relate to God and not to us. Jesus taught us to pray that God's name be sanctified, honoured, respected, that His kingdom come and that His will be done on earth as it is in heaven. Pray for those things first and foremost, let them be the focus of your prayer life, pray for your church, the work of the kingdom, pray for God's name to be honoured in the earth and so on and so forth. When you do this, you are following the divine order for prayer and praying according to God's will. We have a promise in Scripture that any prayer made according to His will is heard and answered by Him. Beautiful stuff. After doing this you can now go on to pray about your own needs.

The second secret is this : petition God for things not on the basis of the problem, but on the basis of His promise. In other words, when you want Him to do something, find out what His heart is on the matter. How do you discover His heart? In His Word. You never know; what you were going to request might be something He has expressly stated His disagreement with and you have only to seek out His Word to find out. The classic example I give is asking in prayer for your neighbour's husband, or wife, as the case may be. He will not give you that. Once you know what God has promised to do, then present your request on the basis of His Word. For instance, you can pray, *'Lord, Your Word says that You are my shepherd, I shall not be in want, so Father, I come to present my needs to You. Thank You Father because I know that You have heard me.'*

Whatever you do, do not try to twist His arm, hoodwink, or blackmail Him into doing anything. Some of us have already tried that; it does not work. Trust me. There is a better way.

Now, you might say, if He has already promised it, how come He has not done it yet? Now you are waxing theological because that is a question great minds have wrestled with for generations. God intervenes in the earth on invitation from a human being. We believe it is because humans were the ones who received dominion from God over the earth. And He intervenes according to His will, not ours. The good news is that His will covers things more beautiful and bountiful than ours. God's will is goodness, kindness, and provision for His children.

Pray in the Spirit

When you were born again, you received the Holy Spirit inside you. Jesus promised that the Holy Spirit would direct us, teach us, instruct us, and show us the things of God. And that includes prayer. The Holy Spirit knows exactly what is going on and what needs to be prayed as well as how. He will direct you into God's Word. He will make you say things in prayer you never imagined. There is a dimension here of prophetic praying, speaking truths by the Spirit that you never knew before.

We are told in the eighth chapter of Romans that we do not know how to pray and what to ask for, and that, consequently, the Holy Spirit helps us to pray. He helps us to pray with groans which cannot be uttered in articulate speech. That is supernatural praying by the Holy Spirit. Be open to it. Be open to praying in other tongues. It is not something strange. It is beautiful and given by God.

When you begin to pray in tongues, throw yourself into it. Pray as often as you can. Paul claimed that he spoke in tongues more than all the people in the Corinthian church. Now that is a lot of speaking. Speak in tongues as you awake, as you sleep, and as you go about your daily activities when you can. We will discuss this some more in the coming chapters.

Speaking in tongues is a precious, divine gift that we must employ consistently and copiously. When you can, spend a few hours praying in tongues and reading the Word. You will experience exponential supernatural growth. The Holy Spirit will turn you into a powerhouse. He will turn you into an intercessor. Prayer will become a lifestyle and you will not be able to do without it. Companionship with God is addictive. I can desire for you no other addiction. Be addicted to the presence of God.

When you pray, believe. Faith is a prerequisite to answered prayer. Jesus specifically told us that when we make a request of God, we should believe that we have received. We believe at the point of asking not when we see the thing happen. He says if we believe we receive, we shall have it. In other words, for you to have what you asked God for, you first have to believe it is done before you see it. How can you believe it is done? Because you know God's heart of love and goodness; because He says to believe. When you have prayed and are waiting to see it happen, spend the time praising God for His goodness, and do not stop believing.

When you pray, persist till the answer comes. There was once a judge who was not a good man. A poor widow sought him out for justice and he was not inclined to favour her cause. Left to him, he would fain have answered the woman. However, she was persistent and finally prevailed upon him because she refused to stop asking. She got what she wanted. Jesus told this story to emphasise two things: one, that we must pray always; two, that we must not give up.

Even an unrighteous judge is moved to answer by persistence. How much more will our kind Father favour the cause of those who will not be deterred, but who continue to look to Him in faith? The devil is the one who intervenes to hinder the manifestation of God's goodness to us and we must resist until he backs off.

So pray, pray and pray. It is impossible to pray too much. There are many things on earth that God wants to change, and He uses the prayers of His people to so do. Indeed 1 Thessalonians 5.17 exhorts us to 'Pray continually.'

*

Scriptures for meditation

Romans 8.26 – 'In the same way the Spirit helps us in our weakness. We do not know what we ought to pray for, but the Spirit himself intercedes for us with groans that words cannot express.'

Matthew 7.11 – 'If you, then, though you are evil, know how to give good gifts to your children, how much more will your Father in heaven give good gifts to those that ask him!'

Luke 18.1 – 'Then Jesus told his disciples a parable to show them that they should always pray and not give up.'

Philippians 4.6 – 'Do not be anxious about anything, but in everything by prayer and petition, with thanksgiving present your requests to God.'

Colossians 4.2 – 'Devote yourselves to prayer, being watchful and thankful.'

1 Timothy 2.8 – 'I want men everywhere, to lift up holy hands in prayer, without anger or disputing.'

James 4.3 – 'When you ask, you do not receive, because you ask with wrong motives, that you may spend what you get on your plesaures.'

James 5.16 – 'Therefore confess your sins to each other and pray for each other so that you may be healed. The prayer of a righteous man is powerful and effective.'

*

Points to ponder

- Make a habit of praying the Word of God.
- Prayer is a habit that will make you. It will make you mighty; it will make you strong; it will make you close to God; it will make you a satisfied Christian.
- If you can say thank you, you can pray.
- It is an unquantifiable privilege to have the ear of God.

Discussion questions

1. Why pray?
2. How does one pray?
3. Explain 'praying in the Sprit'.
4. What hinders prayer?
5. What are the benefits of prayer?

Prayer

Father, thank You for the free access I have to You in prayer.

Lord, as the disciples asked Jesus, I ask you 'Lord, teach me to pray'. I commit to pray faithfully, daily; give me hunger, passion, inspiration and stamina for powerful praying. I want to win great battles in the place of prayer. And I want, above all, to be as near to you as a human is able to be.

5

Be baptised

"Baptism is commanded, and Faith obeys because it is commanded, and thus takes her proper place."

Charles Spurgeon
(Sunday sermon, June 5, 1864,
Metropolitan Tabernacle)

*

'Repent, and be baptised, every one of you, in the name of Jesus Christ for the forgiveness of sins. And you will receive the gift of the Holy Spirit. The promise is for you and your children, and for all who are far off– for all whom the Lord our God will call' (Acts 2.38-39).

The chariot wound steadily through the desert. The lone passenger was a distinguished individual, a man usually kept busy with affairs of state in his native country. Yet he was a pious man and was even now returning from worship in Jerusalem and heading for his homeland. He sat quietly, musing, reading, a puzzled look on his face. How he would love to understand these truths! The words were simple enough; yet, deep within, he knew that he was a long way from penetrating the truths of God's Word. His heart pled that the great God, in His mercy, would open His Word to him.

Still musing, he turned, and came face to face with a stranger walking alongside him, looking at his scroll. 'Do you understand what you are reading?' asked the stranger.

He, in quick response, answered, 'how can I unless someone explains it to me?' Immediately, the stranger, needing no further invitation, mounted the chariot and proceeded to explain the Scriptures to him.

The God of heaven had responded to one lone, hungry soul. The presence of the stranger was no accident. The Holy Spirit had interrupted his activities and given him express instructions. He was to leave where he was and go to this specific place. God had planned this encounter. The stranger looked at the very portion that the man was reading and proceeded to show him the way of salvation in Christ Jesus. He demonstrated that the prophecy of Isaiah, which had so puzzled the man, spoke of Jesus – His sufferings, death, and victory on behalf of man. It was water being poured on thirsty ground. The man received it as the very Word of God and believed.

As the chariot advanced, they came by some water upon which he immediately requested that he be baptised. The stranger, Philip the evangelist, gladly acquiesced. They alighted from the chariot and Philip baptised the man, an official of the court of the Queen of Ethiopia, who went on his way rejoicing in his new faith. You have also had an encounter with the revelation of Jesus, possibly not as dramatic as the official's, but no less valid. Your next step is baptism.

WHAT IS BAPTISM?

The word baptism is a transposition into English of the Greek word 'baptizo', which could imply to dip, to plunge, to dunk; decidedly not theological sounding. The act, though, is profound. It involves taking a new believer and plunging them into water, preferably running water and bringing them out again. The goal is not to cleanse their bodies, as the Apostle Paul points out in one of his letters. Rather it is to testify to their new faith in Christ.

Baptism predated the Christian faith. The Jewish people practised a baptism of repentance; John the Baptist is so named because his primary ministry, which was to prepare the people for the coming of Jesus, focused on calling them to repentance and baptising them. The imagination of generations of children in Sunday School has been fired by images of a rather wild looking man clothed in animal skin thundering against the evils of the religious establishment. His status as a prophet could not be in doubt. He baptised scores of people who came to him in the wilderness, including Jesus, who – though without sin – submitted to baptism to fulfil all righteousness.

Christian baptism differs from Jewish baptism, however, as it follows faith in Jesus. It is done, according to the instructions of Jesus, in the name of the Father, the Son, and the Holy Spirit. The Scriptures relate an occasion in the city of Ephesus, when the Apostle Paul met a group of disciples who had only received the baptism of John. Paul explained the gospel further to them and they were baptised afresh in Christ Jesus.

WHY BE BAPTISED?

If all of this is new to you, or if you were sprinkled as an infant, you may wonder, why be baptised anyway? The most compelling reason is actually the only reason we ever need to do anything: Jesus commanded it. After His resurrection, as the gospel of Matthew relates, Jesus instructed the church to make disciples of all nations, to baptise them and teach them to obey. Then He returned to heaven. The church calls it the Great Commission, and baptism is an integral component of it. Baptism is very closely associated with salvation. It is not a prerequisite for or even a component of salvation; rather, it is the logical sequence to it. Jesus commands it and the Scriptures explain it.

We are baptised because of the significance of baptism. Baptism represents identification, testimony, and admission.

Identification

When a person is plunged into the water and brought out again, they are identifying with the death and resurrection of the Lord.

> 'In him you were also circumcised, in the putting off of the sinful nature, not with a circumcision done by the hands of men but with the circumcision done by Christ, having been buried with him in baptism and raised with him through your faith in the power of God, who raised him from the dead' (Colossians 2.11-12).

Remember, it is through His death and resurrection that we receive salvation; in His death He took our place and underwent the punishment due to us; in His resurrection He defeated death and the devil and took back the dominion over the enemy. Meditate on it as you go into the baptismal waters; consider that you are about to die. When you come out, recognize that you have risen from the dead with victory and dominion over the devil, as you identify with Jesus. The imagery is a powerful one.

Testimony

Public, or even private, baptism is our testimony to the fact that we have stepped out of our old ways into the way of life in Christ Jesus. We acknowledge who He is, we recognise what He has done in our lives, and we bear witness to Him as the only way to God. We proclaim that we are new creatures in Christ Jesus, that we have chosen a new way of life.

Admission

The Holy Spirit is the One who baptises us into the Body of Christ when we believe. It is a spiritual admission into the church that is not visible to the eyes of men. However, in baptism, our identification and testimony also serve to symbolise our membership of the Body of Christ.

The early church was very strong on this point and baptism was a major celebration. The newly baptised believers were symbolically anointed with oil and given white garments to wear as a symbol of their new purity. They were then admitted to full membership in the visible church and allowed to take communion. There have been many baptismal practices in the history of the church. The question then is, how is baptism conducted?

HOW IS BAPTISM DONE?

Baptism is conducted by lowering a person into water and bringing them out again. That sounds straightforward enough, but you probably know people who practice it differently. For evangelical believers, the matter is crystal clear: baptism is by immersion. You are plunged into water and brought up again. Theologically, we are buried with Christ in the plunging under water; we are made alive with Him as we come out of the water. Experientially, Scriptural examples are of people plunged into water. In the early church, baptism was by full-body immersion, and required the use of a lot of water. Concerning John the Baptist, the Scriptures say this:

> 'After this, Jesus and his disciples went out into the Judean countryside, where he spent some time with them, and baptised. Now John also was baptising at Aenon near Salim, because there was plenty of water, and people were coming constantly to be baptised' (John 3.22-23).

It is possible that in later times – and as the Gospel spread to more arid lands – in cases of water scarcity, allowance was made for baptism by pouring or sprinkling. The Didache, an ancient document from an anonymous Christian community dated late-first or early-second centuries (though disputed), leaves out such a possibility.

It recommends in chapter 7 that baptism be preceded by an instruction 'explaining all things', and then it should be done in the name of the Father, Son, and Holy Spirit in flowing water. In the absence of running water, they were to use 'other water', cold, and if that was not possible, warm. Then it says, 'If you have very little, pour water three times on the head in the name of Father and Son and Holy Spirit.'

However, the Jewish and Christian mode of baptism in the Scriptures is by immersion. When there is no circumstance militating against it, it is to be preferred.

WHEN SHOULD I BE BAPTISED?

You may wonder when you should be baptised – immediately after conversion or following a period of instruction. Peter, on the day of Pentecost was asked by the remorseful crowd what they were to do now. His response?

> 'Repent, and be baptised, every one of you, in the name of Jesus Christ for the forgiveness of your sins. And you will receive the gift of the Holy Spirit. The promise is for you and your children, and for all who are far off–for all whom the Lord our God will call' (Acts 2.38-39).

Repentance is a turnaround, a change of belief and direction. It is that which qualifies us for baptism. In the New Testament, the converts were usually baptised immediately; however, those thus baptised were mostly Jewish people or proselytes – persons who already had an understanding of the Scriptures. History tells us that as the church became more Hellenized, prior instruction became an important part of the preparation for baptism. Former pagans came to the faith without any previous knowledge of God, truth, or doctrine. The church needed to have assurance that these new converts were truly saved. The procedure gradually became fairly lengthy, sometimes as long as three years. In many cases, baptism took place once a year at Easter.

We are in an interesting situation today in the church. Many who have come to faith in Christ had been baptised as infants. That was the case for myself and many in my generation. For some, it was clear as they grew up that they shared none of the values of the faith. I was one of those. For the parents it was a matter of securing their offspring against the possibility of hell fire. Baptism had not been preceded by repentance, or by faith in Christ. When we came to Christ as young adults who had been baptised as babies, and found out about baptism by immersion, it was an eye opener. The prerequisite for salvation is faith and repentance. You must have come to faith in Christ and repented of your former way of life. Otherwise, there is no reason to be baptised.

Today, with the proliferation of non-historic churches, another type of situation has emerged. Some persons are baptised as adults somewhat hastily, but they have not professed true faith in Christ. They had started going to church out of some need in their lives and had been baptised. When interrogated, they had little understanding of who Jesus was, and had certainly not made any commitment to follow Him. They were unsaved and yet had been baptised as adults.

That danger today is a very great one. Many are lured into believing that they are on the road to heaven when they are still on the highway to hell. People have come to our church who did not believe that Jesus is the Son of God, that He is the Saviour and only way to God, and who claimed to be Christians, sometimes freshly baptised. Yet they are not born again. We have to explain to them the very basics of the faith, some receive, some argue their way out of the church to another congregation where they can claim to be saved while still denying the risen Lord.

If you join a congregation that requires you to attend a class before baptism, or waits to see the fruits of your conversion, do not fret or fight. Do not change churches because your friend was baptised very quickly in another church. They have good reasons for their stance.

*

Scriptures for meditation

Romans 1.16 – 'I am not ashamed of the gospel, because it is the power of God for the salvation of everyone who believes: first for the Jew, then for the Gentile.'

Matthew 28.19-20 – 'Therefore go and make disciples of all nations, baptising them in the name of the Father, and of the Son, and of the Holy Spirit, and teaching them to obey everything I have commanded you. And surely I am with you always, to the very end of the age. Amen.'

Luke 3.21-22 – 'When all the people were being baptized, Jesus was baptised too. And as he was praying, heaven was opened and the Holy Spirit descended on him in bodily form like a dove . And a voice came from heaven: "You are my Son, whom I love; with you I am well pleased."'

Acts 2.38 – 'Repent, and be baptised, every one of you, in the name of Jesus Christ for the forgiveness of your sins. And you will receive the gift of the Holy Spirit.'

Romans 6.3-5 – 'Or don't you know that all of us who were baptised into Jesus Christ were baptised into his death? We were therefore buried with him through baptism into death, in order that, just as Christ was raised from the dead through the glory of the Father, we too may live a new life. If we have been united with him in his death, we will certainly also be united with him in his resurrection.'

*

Points to ponder

- When a person is plunged into the water and brought out again, they are identifying with the death and resurrection of the Lord.
- It is not a prerequisite for or even a component of salvation; rather, it is the logical sequence to it.
- The Holy Spirit is the One who baptises us into the Body of Christ when we believe.

Discussion questions

1. What is the significance of baptism?
2. How is it done and why?
3. If I was baptised as an infant, why must I be baptised again?
4. What was the significance of the baptism of John?

Prayer

Father, thank You for my new life in Jesus.

Thank You for not waiting for me to be perfect before saving me. I submit to your instructions and present myself for baptism. I invite You to deepen Your work in my life even as I undergo baptism. Give me a powerful revelation of Jesus and of His work of salvation, that I may never take these wonderful things for granted. In Jesus' name. Amen!

6

Receive Holy Spirit baptism

'For John baptised with water, but in a few days you will be baptised with the Holy Spirit' (Acts 1.5).

Decent people were becoming 'born-again Christians'. We thought it a great pity. Normal people suddenly changed and began to attend Bible studies and talk about Jesus; it was quite incomprehensible. How could such a thing hold their interest and attention to the point of them throwing their reputation to the wind and forfeiting the consideration of their peers? It was something of an epidemic, and sometimes it struck its deadly blow close to home.

Shortly after I left university, it was noised abroad that one of my most respected professors had also succumbed to this malady. My worst fears were confirmed as I returned to campus for my transcript. Worse, I found myself buttonholed into a discussion on religion with him and another person who had been ahead of me in school and was now an assistant teacher. We always knew him to be afflicted and so it came as no surprise.

The conversation was odd. I remember insisting that I was also a Christian, pooh-poohing the whole born-again thing, and then the question came: are you baptised in the Holy Spirit? That was new. They explained, and I looked at them incredulously.

'You mean you just start speaking in a language you do not know, just like that, at will?'

'Yes.' They proceeded to give me a thorough explanation of what the Holy Spirit did. That stumped me. My secondary school experience was long forgotten, and it had no theological basis to it. I knew these people; they were a bit excessive with the Bible thing, but they were sensible, real, and had integrity. This was no strange, bizarre spiritual thing. I left there slightly humbled. I could pretend to be a Christian, but I could not pretend to be baptised in the Holy Spirit. I was not a follower of any strange mystery religions that practised demonic languages, and I knew they were not either. I simply did not have room in my worldview for anything mildly supernatural related to Christianity.

Much later, when I got on my knees and gave my life to the Lord in my room, I knew I wanted to be baptised in the Holy Spirit. I particularly wanted to pray in tongues. So I began to pray for it. Nothing happened, although I had begun to read the Bible voraciously. I did not go to church, there were too many Christians (read 'hypocrites') there; at least so I thought. God had mercy on my ignorant self and a friend stopped by one Sunday morning and invited me to church. I thought *Why not?* and went with her. I thoroughly enjoyed myself, but was slightly offended by the speaking in tongues. It was loud, boisterous, lengthy, and I felt left out. These people prayed and worshipped, singing in tongues with every fibre of their being. I felt it was alienating for people who did not speak in tongues.

This time, unlike in secondary school, I did not try to fake it. I knew better at that point. I wanted the real thing. The next week, my friend did not come back. It might have been due to something I said (I might have complained about the tongues). But I got up on Sunday morning and went to another friend's house and suggested she go with me to church. I had a plan. She came with me.

At the end of the service, an altar call for salvation was made. I did not respond because I was already saved. Then came a second call for people who needed to be filled with the Holy Spirit. I jumped up, took my friend by the hand, and we went forward. We were ushered into a room where they proceeded to share the gospel with us again to make sure we were truly saved. We prayed to receive the Lord, they taught briefly on the Holy Spirit, and we prayed. I was Spirit-filled immediately and began to speak in tongues. To say I was ecstatic is an understatement. That was the reason I went back to the church, I had seen them make the call the previous week.

When I returned home, everyone was out. It was perfect. I spent the entire afternoon praying in tongues, it was as if heaven had come down. That was almost thirty years ago, and I have been praying in tongues every day since then and walking in relationship with the Holy Spirit.

I am so glad that I was not so offended that I refused to go back the next Sunday. So glad I did not become a mortal enemy of tongue speakers, as has unfortunately been the case for some who 'sought' at some point and did not receive. Since my early twenties, barely six months after my conversion, I have lived outside my home country. I have been a good distance from family, with very little personal pastoral input or mentoring into my life over the years. I believe the Holy Spirit and the grace of praying in other tongues is the reason I am in the faith today, and in the ministry, in a nation where many lose their faith on arrival. The Holy Spirit has illuminated the Word of God to me;. He has helped me to pray myself out of very difficult situations. He has shown me the way to go. He has worked miracles in my life. He is very precious to me.

JESUS THE BAPTISER

One of the remarkable things that John the Baptist said about Jesus was that He was the One who would baptise in the Holy Spirit. We are left waiting and wondering throughout the ministry of Jesus. We see Him moving in the power of the Spirit; we see even His disciples to some extent moving in the power of the Spirit as He sent them out to minister in the villages and towns of Israel. They came back excited at all that God had done through them, yet they were not yet baptised in the Holy Spirit. Then, He said two things prior to His departure. In Mark 16, He announced that specific supernatural signs would be displayed through those who believed in Him. One of these was that they would speak in new tongues (languages they had not learnt):

> 'He said to them, 'Go into all the world and preach the good news to all creation. Whoever believes and is baptised will be saved, but whoever does not believe will be condemned. And these signs will accompany those who believe: In my name they will drive out demons; they will speak in new tongues; they will pick up snakes with their hands; and when they drink deadly poison, it will not hurt them at all; they will place their hands on sick people, and they will get well'" (Mark 16.15-18).

Now that may have seemed rather unlikely to some. He also said, as recorded in the first chapter of Acts, that His disciples were to wait in Jerusalem because they would soon be baptised in the Holy Spirit. And He kept His word. On the day of Pentecost, tongues of fire alighted on the heads of the individuals gathered in the Upper Room, their place of prayer. They heard a sound like the rushing of a mighty wind, and they were filled (baptised) with the Holy Spirit.

When Jesus gave the promise of the Spirit's coming, He connected it with power. He said that the disciples would receive power to be witnesses for Him. And that is what happened. They became bold, audacious and began to preach the Gospel fearlessly. They began to demonstrate the supernatural power of God. They healed people, raised people from the dead, delivered those who were oppressed by evil spirits etc. The Holy Spirit will give you the same boldness so you can witness fearlessly as well. In every generation, believers in Christ receive the same Holy Spirit for the same purpose – to be witnesses for Jesus.

Consequently, every Christian who has received the baptism of the Holy Spirit is able to function in supernatural power and be an effective witness. That power is used by God to touch people's lives, to heal, to deliver, to convict and to save. Indeed, the apostle Paul stated without qualms in writing to the church at Corinth that when he preached the gospel to them it was not with sweet sounding human words, rather with a demonstration of the Spirit and power. That is how we must preach the Gospel today. So pray to be endued with power, pray for spiritual sensitivity so that you can follow the Holy Spirit's direction and be an effective witness.

> *God uses acts of power to communicate His truth and to arrest men's attention*

When the disciples received the Holy Spirit on the day of Pentecost, they began to speak supernaturally in languages they had not learnt. The baptism in the Holy Spirit and speaking in tongues (languages) was Jesus' idea and proceeds from Him. Do not make the mistake of assuming that those who do not speak in tongues do not have the Holy Spirit. Not so. If you are born again, you are no stranger to the Holy Spirit. It was He who touched you beforehand to give you conviction of sin, and on your profession of faith baptised you into the church. He has come to indwell you.

There is a greater dimension of power, intimacy, and access to the spirit realm that praying in tongues by the Holy Spirit affords the believer. You are supernaturally made able by God to speak words that you did not learn, a 'language' that flows out of your spirit that your mind does not comprehend. It is a powerful prayer and praise tool for the believer. There are different dimensions to speaking in tongues. They could be human languages that are identifiable, or what the Apostle Paul calls tongues of angels. It does not replace the Word of God; it is yet another powerful way whereby God helps His people to overcome and live supernaturally in the world.

You do not qualify for the baptism in the Holy Spirit because you are spiritual, but because you are saved. What counts is the use you make of this tremendous gift. It is not the sign of your perfection; it is a tool for your perfecting. Remember, the Holy Spirit is God. He is on the earth to help us. Whatever your theological background, it is important to be open to anything that comes from Him. If He gives it, it is good.

Are there any biblical examples? Why speak in tongues anyway if you can be a perfectly decent Christian without speaking in tongues? Who can speak in tongues?

SPEAKING IN TONGUES – BIBLICAL INSTANCES

Many years ago, I sat at table at a high-level official dinner reception, and the conversation veered to spiritual matters. It was a most unlikely place for such to happen and I found myself fielding questions about speaking in tongues. None of the people at table were believers, yet they were captivated by the topic. It seemed totally 'otherworldly' to them, a supernatural dimension to Christianity they had never thought possible in our day. One of the questions, unsurprisingly, was, 'Do you speak in tongues?'

I was glad to respond, 'Yes, I do.' They looked at me with interest and amazement. And I realised my partaking of this otherwise 'strange' phenomenon had made it more real to them and hopefully less incredible.

People often ask, 'If I am baptised in the Holy Spirit, will I speak in tongues?' I do not know if you will, but I know you will be able to. Sometimes people choose not to. They shut their minds to the possibility or are afraid of what people around them will think, particularly those who don't believe in tongues. In such cases, they often do not speak in tongues. They may even demonstrate significant Holy Spirit power in their ministries. But if you are open, you will be able to. Jesus said the Father would give the Holy

Spirit to those who asked Him because of His goodness. Any gift of God that He promises, He gives.

Once in church, I prayed for a young woman to be baptised in the Holy Spirit and I knew it was done. However, this young woman did not speak in tongues. I had three options: conclude that she was not baptised; conclude she was, but tongues were unnecessary; or conclude that something was hindering her speaking in tongues even though she had been baptised. I told her to go home where she was more relaxed than in church and begin to praise and thank God for baptising her in the Holy Spirit. She did as I said. The next time I saw her, she was radiant. She testified that as she praised God at home, she began to speak very naturally in tongues.

Having prayed with many over the years to receive the baptism in the Holy Spirit, I know that there is sometimes a sense of strangeness in our perception of this gift. Some are uncomfortable about speaking words they do not understand. Some may even have been told that speaking in tongues is of the devil. Others believe that you cannot speak in tongues at will, even after being baptised; you must wait for a special feeling to speak. Even among people who do believe, there is sometimes rigid, religious tradition stifling this wonderful gift.

I like to take such people through a few simple instances in the Scriptures where people received the baptism in the Holy Spirit to show how real and simple it is. It strengthens their faith that this is indeed a God-sent blessing for them.

Let us look at some of the instances when people were baptised in the Holy Spirit in Scripture.

Pentecost

In the second chapter of the book of Acts, the event that triggered off the beginnings and subsequent expansion of the church was the baptism in the Holy Spirit. As Jack Hayford puts it in his book, The Beauty of Spiritual Language, 'the church began speaking in tongues the same day it came into being.' It caused a commotion in that part of the city. The disciples of Jesus were in an upper room praying and the Holy Spirit came upon them. There was a mighty wind and tongues of fire came to rest on their heads. He overwhelmed them with power and they began to speak in other tongues, languages they had never learnt. When it came to the attention of the people gathered in Jerusalem, an uproar ensued. Certainly some, if not all, the 'tongues' they spoke were the languages of the people present. The people marvelled, and Peter seized the opportunity to preach a powerful message. Thousands were subsequently saved.

Cornelius and company

Another occasion was in the house of a man called Cornelius. God had instructed Peter through a vision to go to

Cornelius' house, though he was a Gentile. Cornelius himself had earlier been instructed by God to send for Peter so he could preach the gospel to him and his family. Thus, Cornelius had gathered his household together, and they were eager to hear the Word of the Lord. Peter obeyed and went to Cornelius' house with the men sent to fetch him. He spoke the Word of God to the people gathered, and while he was still speaking to them, the Bible tells us that the 'Holy Spirit fell' on them. They were baptised in the Spirit and spoke in tongues. The Jewish disciples realised the Gentiles had been baptised with the Spirit because they heard them 'speak with tongues and magnify God': 'While Peter was still speaking these words, the Holy Spirit came on all who heard the message. The circumcised believers who had come with Peter were astonished that the gift of the Holy Spirit had been poured out even on the Gentiles' (Acts 10.44-47).

The twelve from Ephesus

On a visit to Ephesus, the Apostle Paul met a group of twelve men who claimed to be disciples. On further enquiry, he discovered that they had not received the Holy Spirit and knew nothing about Him. They only knew the baptism of John. Paul proceeded to teach them about Jesus. They believed, and he baptised them in the name of the Lord. Afterwards, he laid hands on them and we are told: 'When Paul placed his hands on them, the Holy Spirit came on them, and they spoke in tongues and prophesied' (Acts 19.6).

Paul spoke in tongues a lot

After Paul's Damascus road experience and his resultant conversion, hands were laid on him to be filled with the Holy Spirit. And we know from his letter to the church in Corinth that he spoke in tongues, a lot. Indeed, he claimed to speak in tongues more than the entire church.

Miracle in Samaria

Philip the evangelist went to Samaria and set the town on fire, spiritually speaking. Mass conversions took place; healings and miracles were everywhere. The Apostles got wind of this, and they sent Peter and John over to minister the Holy Spirit to the new converts. Acts Chapter 8 states:

> 'When the Apostles in Jerusalem heard that Samaria had accepted the word of God, they sent Peter and John to them. When they arrived, they prayed for them that they might receive the Holy Spirit, because the Holy Spirit had not yet come upon any of them; they had simply been baptized into the name of the Lord Jesus' (v. 14-16).

I believe this means that they had not received the baptism in the Holy Spirit. So Peter and John laid hands on them in prayer. Did they speak in tongues when they received? It is not said, but it is extremely likely that they did.. There was, apparently, a visible sign that they had received the Holy Spirit when hands were laid on them. This sign was so obvious that one crooked fellow who was there, a certain Simon, wanted to bribe the Apostles to give him the same power of conferring the Holy Spirit on people.

WHAT WILL IT DO FOR ME?

Now that we have established the fact that speaking in tongues is a good thing, what exactly does it do for you?

Worship

When we speak in tongues, we magnify God. The Spirit of God has given us this wonderful way to offer God perfect praise. Irrespective of the prevailing vogue in worship style or music, irrespective of your own musical savvy or lack thereof, you can rest assured that you can praise and magnify God as well as anyone else. Indeed, when we speak in tongues, we magnify God as we ought. We say to Him those things we ought to say; we sing, led by the Spirit of God. It is beautiful.

Communication of mysteries with God

> 'For anyone who speaks in a tongue does not speak to people but to God. Indeed, no one understands them; they utter mysteries by the Spirit.' (1 Corinthians 14.2)

One other delightful thing that we discover about speaking in tongues is that when we speak in tongues we speak mysteries to God. I am like a child with this one. Human knowledge is finite. I am often supremely conscious of all that I do not know, but by the Holy Spirit, as I speak in other tongues, I can speak to the Most High God, Creator of all things, about eternal truths and mysteries. And I can expect Him to give me understanding of some of these things as I go along in my relationship with Him. After all, His Word does say that the things God has prepared for those who love Him far exceed anything we have ever seen or heard. It also says that He has revealed these things to us by His Spirit. Absolutely splendid!

Building up

When you speak in tongues, the Bible says, you build yourself up. Today, almost everyone has a mobile phone, sometimes a tablet, often a laptop; different devices with different functions, but one thing is common: they must be charged as the power runs out.

Human beings, too, often need a recharge of fire and power. Speaking in tongues recharges our batteries; that is what it means to build yourself up. Unlike the device charging, however, we are not voltage or capacity bound. As we charge, we surge. There is no overheating and no need for a circuit breaker. As we can keep charging, the power continues to increase; our strength grows exponentially as well as our sensitivity to the spirit realm of God.

Edification also means the capacity to withstand adversity; the stronger we are, the more able we are to overcome the things that oppose us. 'He who speaks in a tongue edifies himself, but he who prophesies edifies the church. I would like every one of you to speak in tongues, but I would rather have you prophesy' (1 Corinthians 14.4-5).

Supernatural praying

The Holy Spirit helps us to pray in a supernatural manner. Romans Chapter eight explains to us that, given our limited knowledge of the content and manner of prayer, the Holy Spirit helps us to pray. He does this by enabling us to utter sounds in prayer that – though they do not make sense to us – are extremely effective in the spirit. We can easily surmise that when we pray in tongues by the Holy Spirit, He is enabling us to overcome the deficiency occasioned by our ignorance. Things happen that we are unaware of; situations are not all they appear; there are underlying factors that elude us, so we need help. Were we to put our case like a lawyer based solely on the information available to us, we would lose our case. But the One who sees the invisible and knows the unexpected steps in and helps us to deal with every situation effectively in the Spirit.

HOW DOES ONE RECEIVE?

You want to take your time to mull over the Scriptures on the baptism in the Holy Spirit. You can pray in your home and ask God to baptise you in the Holy Spirit. I would encourage you to ask for prayer in your local church or from persons you trust who do believe in speaking in tongues. Receive by faith. Trust God.

There is no need for drama or theatrics. As you receive prayer, believe, and simply open your mouth and begin to speak in tongues. Sometimes it will come gushing out; that's the way it was for me. One of the finest experiences I have had in this area was in ministering in Colombia. I called for people who wanted to be baptised in the Holy Spirit and many came forward. One of them was a pastor I had met earlier, a very gracious man. I was surprised that he was not baptised in the Holy Spirit. As I prayed for him, there was a wonderful outpouring and he broke out in tongues without the slightest hindrance. He spoke eloquently and powerfully as one who had prayed in tongues for many years.

Sometimes you are voicing simple syllables. And you may even be wondering if it is the real deal. If it is not your language, it most likely is. There are those who may not speak in tongues immediately. As I explained earlier, this is no cause for concern. Once you have discounted the possibility of or dealt with demonic hindrances, trust God. Keep thanking God and the tongues will come.

One Sunday, I spoke to a visitor at the end of the service. The woman was in town for the weekend and had attended our service on her mother's recommendation. The mother had visited a few times with her husband when they were in town and had been powerfully touched. As we spoke, she poured out her heart that she wanted more fire in her Christian life. We spoke about the baptism in the Holy Spirit. She admitted that even though she desired it, her traditional religious environment and Bible School had affected her thinking. Though she had seen the change in her family, she still felt torn, but she was in such a dry place spiritually that she wanted prayer.

I prayed with her, but she did not speak in tongues right away. I encouraged her not to fret about it, but to rest in the Lord. She was to go home, and in the comfort of her home, thank the Lord for baptising her in the Holy Spirit and ask that she be enabled to pray in tongues. Several weeks later, the mother was back in the service and insisted on telling me what happened afterwards. Her daughter did as I told her, and she had a powerful encounter with the Holy Spirit. Now she speaks in tongues continuously, her spiritual life is blossoming, and she is full of joy. Her family has been positively affected and she has had some tremendous testimonies of answered prayer.

God will do the same for you. Don't hesitate to pray in tongues every single day. And as you pray in tongues, listen inside. Sometimes God will give you an understanding of what you were speaking in the Holy Spirit, sometimes not. Stay focused on developing your prayer life, on developing your relationship with the Holy Spirit. Do not forget to pray in your own language as well. We are encouraged to do both.

> 'For if I pray in a tongue, my spirit prays, but my mind is unfruitful. So what shall I do? I will pray with my spirit, but I will also pray with my mind; I will sing with my spirit, but I will also sing with my mind' (1 Corinthians 14.14-15).

Shalom!

*

Scriptures for meditation

Acts 1.5 – 'For John baptised with water, but in a few days you will be baptised with the Holy Spirit.'

Acts 2.1-4 – 'When the day of Pentecost came, they were all together in one place. Suddenly a sound like the blowing of a violent wind came from heaven and filled the whole house where they were sitting. They saw what seemed to be tongues of fire that separated and came to rest on each of them. All of them were filled with the Holy Spirit and began to speak in other tongues as the Spirit enabled them.'

Luke 3.16 – 'John answered them all, "I baptise you with water. But one more powerful than I will come, the thongs of whose sandals I am not worthy to untie. He will baptise you with the Holy Spirit and fire."'

Acts 19.2 – ' and asked them, "Did you receive the Holy Spirit when you believed?" They answered, "No, we have not even heard that there is a Holy Spirit."'

Jude 1.20 – 'But you, dear friends, build yourselves up in your most holy faith and pray in the Holy Spirit.'

Acts 10.44-46 – 'While Peter was still speaking these words, the Holy Spirit came on all who heard the message. The circumcised believers who had come with Peter were astonished, because the gift of the Holy Spirit had been poured out even on the Gentiles. For they heard them speaking in tongues and praising God.'

*

Points to ponder

- The Holy Spirit helps us to pray in a supernatural manner.
- You do not qualify for the baptism in the Holy Spirit because you are spiritual, but because you are saved.
- Human beings, too, often need a recharge of fire and power. Speaking in tongues recharges our batteries; that is what it means to build yourself up.

Discussion questions

1. What is the baptism in the Holy Spirit?
2. How important is it to speak in tongues?
3. How do you receive?
4. How often should you pray in tongues?

Prayer

Father, I desire more of You.

I want everything that You have for me. Thank You for the baptism in the Holy Spirit. I ask You Lord Jesus to baptise me in the Holy Spirit. I renounce all sin and wickedness. Lord, I commit wholly to follow You. Fill me to overflowing Lord and enable me to pray in the supernatural language of the Spirit. Endue me with the power of the Holy Spirit. In Jesus' name. Amen!

7

Serve

> "It is God's will that every believer without exception, whatever be his position in life, gives himself wholly to live and work for God."
>
> Andrew Murray
> (Working for God)

*

'Therefore, my dear brothers, stand firm. Let nothing move you. Always give yourselves in fully to the work of the Lord, because you know that your labour in the Lord is not in vain' (1 Corinthians 15.58).

The disciples of Jesus were very much like us. James and John were brothers who used to be fishermen, but gave it all up to follow Jesus. Then one day, James and John had an idea. It occurred to them that perhaps they ought to jump ahead of the others and stake a claim for supremacy in the coming kingdom. So they requested the positions next to Jesus when He would come in His glory. As was to be expected, the other disciples were indignant, but not because they thought such presumption unworthy of disciples of the Son of God. Rather, they did not take kindly to being supplanted.

Jostling for prominence is inherent to fallen humanity. Here is how Jesus responded. He proceeded to give them a lesson in what constituted true greatness, and it would behove us to pay attention to this unusual perspective. The Gentile rulers, Jesus said, were authoritarian and lorded it over the people. His disciples were not to be so. Rather, those who wanted to be great, He said, must serve. Those who wanted to be first must choose to be the slave of others. So far, so good ... well, perhaps. But there was more.

Even the Son of Man, He said, did not come to be served, but to serve, and to give His life as a ransom for many[1]. Jesus personified and lived a life of total service, giving of Himself continually and unconditionally to other people. James and John and the other feuding disciples were duly chastened. Quite possibly they were left wondering what they had signed up for. They wanted to be 'big men' but are told they must be servants.

Not so different from us, were they? The good news is that those men did change. They ended up grasping the significance of what they had been entrusted with. All of them, save Judas, ended up living amazing lives of service and leaving their mark on the earth. James went to his death serving Jesus. John, the beloved John, history tells us, outlived them all and even at a ripe old age, he was still serving God and honouring Jesus. It is very heartwarming and encouraging to see how God changes hearts. What Jesus said to them applies to us all.

The next pointer to running your race in order to win the prize is service. A Christian has a duty to serve God. It must be his set purpose. He is offered a grand opportunity to live life no longer in service to the devil or to self, but to live a life of significance in service to God. Some need no prodding and literally beg for the opportunity to be useful to God as soon as they receive salvation. For others, it is a novel idea that takes some getting used to. They begin to wonder what they have signed up for. Still others remain oblivious or indifferent, wasting their time on endeavours

---

1. (Mark 10.42-44).

that lack eternal significance. The change witnessed in the disciples is an encouragement to all.

WHAT IS SERVING GOD?

When people truly understand redemption, they will be falling over themselves to make themselves useful to God.

To serve is

- to make oneself of use to achieve a purpose
- to discharge a duty
- to assist in a task
- to acquit oneself of one's responsibilities
- to comply with a command
- to meet the needs of someone
- to contribute to something

Jesus says that those who would be great must become a servant of all. In other words, one must do away with one's own preferences, prerogatives, and priorities; and instead focus on the need at hand. He turns our understanding of greatness on its head. He Himself embodied this principle, as is demonstrated throughout the gospels and described in the second chapter of Paul's letter to the Philippian church. Jesus ceded His glory, preferences, and prerogatives. He stepped down into a subservient position in order to serve the purpose of the Father to redeem His creation. Consequently, as the same chapter explains, God has exalted Him and given Him the name that is above every other name. At His name, every knee will bow and every tongue will confess that Jesus is Lord, to the glory of God the Father. He made Himself nothing (of no reputation) and God made Him everything.

Jesus discharged all His duties; He was focused and relentless, and paid the ultimate price to create the right conditions for humanity to be saved. His coming to earth was purposeful and His life one long mission of generosity. His death was but the culmination of a life of service. It involved challenges, pain, suffering, even physical fatigue as a human. He submitted to human rules of living, and He persevered and never stopped serving. Think about what Jesus said to the disciples after James and John's impertinent request. Work them through your mind; they entail a fundamental paradigm shift for most of us. It is as that shift takes place that our lives will become of use to God.

The next thing you need to do with this new life is to begin to serve God diligently and generously. That is why Paul says:

> 'Therefore, my dear brothers, stand firm. Let nothing move you. Always give yourselves fully to the work of the Lord, because you know that your labour in the Lord is not in vain' (1 Corinthians 15.58).

Did you notice the words 'fully' and 'labour'? How wonderful that in the kingdom of God, your effort is never wasted. Nothing you do is in vain. Scripture clearly shows that God's ultimate plan is not to devote His time to cooing over us as newborn babies for the rest of our lives. Rather, He offers us the privilege of contributing to His grand purpose of reconciling the world to Himself. He invites us to live such that our lives will add value to the kingdom – liberated from obsession with self, service to self, and its attendant dissatisfaction. That is what gives true happiness, and true greatness.

> *As a child of God, you are offered a grand opportunity to live life no longer in service to the devil or to self, but to live a life of significance in service to God.*

WHY SERVE GOD?

'If my labour is not in vain, what purpose does it serve?' you may ask, and 'Why should I serve, even if I have no pretensions to greatness? Is my specific contribution that important? Does it matter? Why serve God then?'

Because it honours Him

We serve God to glorify Him. According to First Peter, chapter four verse eleven, the believer should serve God with the strength that God gives so that God will be glorified in all things by Jesus Christ. Serving God means honouring God and giving Him glory. It means that we honour Him enough to put our lives at His disposal. We serve those we respect naturally, so not serving Him is disrespectful of Him.

Also, the fruit of our service should speak good of God and contribute to God achieving His purpose in the earth, the redemption of humanity and of creation.

Because of who we are

Our identity influences our conduct. When we truly know who we have been made into through the new birth, we understand that not serving God would be an anomaly. What is it about our identity that makes serving God a given?

We belong to God and owe Him all

Truth be told, if He did not call us to serve Him, we should beg to be allowed to serve Him simply because we are grateful. Think of it. The very breath that we have is the result of His giving. The new life in Christ is a result of His service and His giving. Without Him, we are not. We are creatures of His making and His saving, utterly dependent on His grace for every breath, for every day, for every gift, and for every capacity. It is one of the great privileges of the new birth to be able to serve God and our fellows as we ought, to put our all at His disposal.

Jesus' words are not an invitation to serve others with the sole purpose of becoming great; they simply mean that greatness is found in service. Consequently, we are all called to greatness because we are all called to serve – to serve God, and to serve people. Indeed, true Christian maturity is gauged, among other things, by your degree of commitment to service, to advancing the cause of Christ.

We are ambassadors of the kingdom

If you have read the first book in this series REBORN, A New Identity, you would have read the chapter on citizens and ambassadors of the kingdom. As a child of God, you have been granted full citizenship in God's kingdom and ambassadorial status. As an ambassador, you represent the interests of the kingdom of God and work to advance the cause of your ruler God in the earth. You are on Team Jesus. Astounding ... or perhaps for you it sounds like a tall order. No fear; God has made it possible for you, irrespective of your ability and background, to be effective in His service and live a glorious life of giving to others. Paul, writing to the church in Ephesus and to us, states:

> 'It was he who gave some to be apostles, some to be prophets, some to be evangelists, and some to be pastors and teachers, to prepare God's people for works of service, so that the body of Christ may be built up until we all reach unity in the faith and in the knowledge of the Son of God

and become mature, attaining to the whole measure of the fulness of Christ' (Ephesians 4.11-13).

Do you see that besides being called to works of service, God's people are also equipped, built up with the rest of the church, and able to grow? God has made special provision through His ministry gifts for you to be properly trained, and you need it, to do 'works of service'. He has not asked you to make bricks without straw. All that is required is for you to acknowledge the call to serve and say yes, today, even as you read this book.

We have worthy examples to follow. We stand on the shoulders of great men. Paul the Apostle was one such remarkable individual. He was a shining example of service. He demonstrated uncommon faithfulness, and considered – as we also should – that it was a singular privilege to be called to service:

> 'I thank Christ Jesus our Lord, who has given me strength, that he considered me faithful, appointed me to his service' (1 Timothy 1.12).

Oh, how I covet that, to be considered faithful and to be appointed to His service on that basis.

We are stewards of God

In the famous parable of the talents (Matthew 25.14-30), Jesus tells the story of a man who went away on a trip and committed resources into the hands of his servants.

Three in number, each received resources commensurate with their capacity. On his return, the master found that the first two had utilised the resources and committed to them wisely. They had invested their 'talents' and obtained a high yield. The master had been enriched by their faithfulness; they were duly commended.

The third individual, on the other hand, had been slothful and indifferent to his master's interests. He had stowed away the resources and simply handed back to the master what he had been originally given without any yield for the master. The master was furious – not only at his slothfulness but even more at his total indifference to the master's interests. 'Well then,' he said, 'you should have put my money on deposit with the bankers, so that when I returned I would have received it back with interest.' And so the third servant fell under judgement while the others received greater responsibilities.

We are those servants in the story. We have received stewardship of the Master's resources in different forms. These are to be developed and utilised to advance the Master's interests and further His purpose on the earth. Every life in Christ must make a difference in the earth. If we live for ourselves alone, we are of all men most miserable. If the vast resources God endowed us with are left unutilised, we fail as stewards. I encourage you to live well. To live well is to serve God; it is to conform our lives and devote our capacity to His glory. When we live well, we die well.

Paul lived well. Many may not think so because of the hardships he had to endure, but he patterned his life after the blueprint the Lord showed him after their encounter on the road to Damascus. He was very vocal about the fact that his life meant fruitful service to the Master, nothing else; it was either living and serving, or dying. Living without serving was not an option. A truly remarkable life. Paul died well.

Before he died, Paul wrote to his son in the faith, Timothy, and explained to him that he was satisfied that he had discharged his duties most honourably. Consequently, he was eager for the reward that awaited him on the other side. He was eager to receive the crown of righteousness. We serve God because we have received a trust. Paul's gratitude was that he was considered faithful and thus entrusted with the service.

Because there is an eternal purpose

Intrinsic to God's purpose in saving us is that we would be reconciled to Him and that we would serve Him. We do not serve merely because we are grateful. In other words, we do not serve out of the goodness of our hearts, subject to the ebbs and flows of our lives. Serving is a part of God's eternal purpose and salvation package. The Bible puts it this way: *'we are God's workmanship, created in Christ Jesus to do good works'* (Ephesians 2.10a).

Not only were you created in Christ Jesus to do good works, but even before you came to know the Lord, God had been preparing some specific things for you to do when the time came. Hard to fathom, isn't it? But that is precisely what Scripture says. The same passage in Ephesians points out that those good works were *'prepared in advance for us to do'* (Ephesians 2.10b).

Think of it. What does this mean for you personally? It means that God had you in mind long before you came to Jesus, that He prepared work for you to do for Him when you would come to Jesus. And this is part of your normal life as a Christian. This work is supposed to be abundant, consistent, regular, unceasing.

> *To live well is to serve God; it is to conform our lives and devote our capacity to His glory. When we live well, we die well.*

As we saw earlier, in writing to the Christians at Corinth the Apostle Paul enjoined them to give themselves fully to the work of the Lord. Set your mind to work for God; find out what He wants you to do and do it with all your heart. In the same letter, Paul reminds them that their labour in the Lord is not in vain. Whatever you do for God carries rewards.

WHAT DOES IT ENTAIL?

Jesus left us a mandate before leaving the earth. He made it very clear what every believer should be doing. We are mandated to preach the gospel and to make disciples, baptising them and teaching them to obey Jesus. This will involve healing the sick as well as different types of signs and wonders, as we see in the book of Acts. These activities and the supporting activities that make them possible are the tasks before every believer.

Jesus is doing this through the church, hence kingdom service will be rooted in the local church, though not restricted to it. We function and serve in community, in a strategic and coordinated fashion. I will refrain from giving you a catalogue of services to be rendered to the Most High. I will leave that to you and your spiritual leaders under the direction of the Holy Spirit. Suffice it to say that each of us has a calling, a gift – spiritual or natural – time, resources, and physical energy that can be used for the advancement of the kingdom.

We are not dealing here with secular employment done to the glory of God in terms of working diligently and being a good person at work and a credit to the faith. Might I suggest that most secular employment is done to the glory of our bank accounts and for our satisfaction if, indeed, it is a job we find satisfaction in. Rather, I speak of activities that directly result in the advancement of the kingdom, the conversion of souls, discipling, and building the local church. Some of this can and should occur at work – conversion and discipling for instance. Some of it can be helped by work – giving for instance. Yet the job itself is not directly serving God.

This misconception, in my view, is one reason why many churches lack workers. Few Christians share their faith with a view to winning souls, and many feel imposed upon when asked to participate in kingdom-related activities. They think, 'Well, I work full time, I glorify God with my work, but the church is the pastor's job. I do my job without asking him to participate, so he should do his. I attend church to be blessed and give him money.' Not so … not so at all.

What you do will also depend on your church context to some extent. In a new church, you may not have the luxury of doing the very thing that you feel called to … but be expected to do any and everything that needs to be done. Jump in and do it; you may even need to learn new skills to meet a need in the church for which the church would otherwise have to pay a lot of money. That is how we make ourselves useful.

In the early days of a church, members may need to learn to do everything: worship, sound, video, graphics, website development, contract negotiation, etc. As things evolve, people can focus more on their specific gifting. The important thing, as Jesus said, is to make ourselves useful to others, not to be first. Whatever you do that lightens the burden on your leaders and Pastors is your service to God.

What do you do? Whatever needs to be done. Street evangelism? Why not? You are timid? It can be overcome. When we put no limitations on our usefulness, we become extremely successful in serving God. The kingdom is our Father's business; we all have a stake in its welfare. The next question is, what attitudes come into play as I serve God.

THE RIGHT ATTITUDE FOR KINGDOM SERVICE

You know the well-worn cliché, 'your attitude determines your altitude'. It makes for rousing preaching but is nevertheless true. Many years ago when we started our church, one of the people who came on board asked me at the very first meeting they attended, 'What can I do to help?' I was touched. So many show up for what they can take, but here was someone who wanted to give something. Yet I found that they were not very helpful because everything seemed too hard for them, too complicated, or too difficult. I spent hours dealing with them. It took a lot of patience to finally get some usefulness out of them. It was not until many years later that they admitted that they had done things out of a sense of duty but had not been wholly dedicated. That certainly affected their usefulness and ability in serving.

Wholeheartedness

To serve God fully, there is need for wholeheartedness. Jesus embodied single-minded devotion to the call; His whole heart and soul was in it. It was what He lived for. Consequently, when He met the woman by the well of Samaria, despite his tiredness, He ministered at length to her. Interestingly, by the time He was done, the disciples wondered if someone had brought Him food, and He truthfully and tellingly replied, *'My food, [said Jesus] is to do the will of him who sent me and to finish his work' (John 4.34).* Whatever we do in serving God, it must be with all our hearts, even when things get tough.

Responsibility mindset

One major attitude shift required as we serve God is to switch from the entitlement mentality to the responsibility mindset. Jesus told a very telling story in this regard, as related in Luke 17. He painted a scenario for His disciples: say they had a servant with a set of responsibilities. He is out ploughing or tending sheep, and then he comes into the house. What next? Will they have him sit down and eat? Or would they have him finish his work – preparing supper, waiting on the master while he ate etc, after which he would attend to his own meal? And when the servant had complied, would they give him special thanks for doing as he was told? The answer is no, as he would essentially have merely discharged the duties for which he was hired.

Similarly, Jesus says we, after doing whatever it is we do in the service of God should not be expecting accolades or expecting to be feted in one way or other. Our attitude should be that we have simply done our duty. We have done no more than is our responsibility to do.

> 'So you also, when you have done everything you were told to do, should say, "We are unworthy servants; we have only done our duty"' (Luke 17.10).

Humility

Learn to serve, in humility, considering every task an honour and a privilege. We live in a selfish age and God wants to strip the selfishness and self absorption out of us. Let Him see you as one serving, not one demanding to be served or demanding royal treatment in the church. Some will not serve, but want to be in charge.

Whatever your status in the world, you are not more important than any other sister or brother in the church. Submit to the people in charge – be they poorer than you, smaller than you, or younger than you. When you have done what you were told to do, whatever it is, you have done no more than you ought. God has shown you immense favour in saving you. Demonstrate your allegiance and sense of responsibility by serving Him outrageously without seeking anything in return, neither praise nor profit.

Neither praise nor profit?

Yes, neither praise, as we have seen, nor profit. A person was asked by a member of his family as he did some work for his church, 'Are you being paid for this?' He made it clear it was a privilege to serve God. We should be glad God does not insist on a reciprocal financial exchange for services mutually rendered, or we would all go to hell; no one can pay Him for salvation. We owe Him forever. Anything we do for Him, we do in His debt.

This person, despite highly inauspicious beginnings, was set on course for a beautiful life. He had literally been brought back from the brink of death and his entire life turned around by what God had done for him in that very church. Could such a person rightfully demand payment for doing those things for the salvation of others that he had benefited from freely?

Believers attend the same church for years and benefit from other people's selfless giving and service, and some will still not serve unless they are paid. Can a Christian singer charge for a CD? Yes. Should they insist on payment to be on the worship team? A thousand times no. When we will not sing unless we are paid, or work for God unless we are paid, we lose the opportunity to demonstrate gratitude, to give back, and to sow freely into other lives.

The Lord never fails to honour His own. Jesus' words still stand: *'Give, and it will be given to you'* and, *'It is more blessed to give than to receive' (Luke 6.38, Acts 20.35).* We acknowledge that there is room for some to receive remuneration who work full-time in the ministry. The labourer, as the Scriptures say, is worthy of his hire.

If one day you are called to be a minister of the gospel, know that there is full scriptural support for those who preach and teach God's Word full time and lead God's people to be supported financially for doing so by their local congregation and others who choose to. That enables them to give all their time to the work of God. But it does not entitle them to name their price before they preach, as some Christian speakers do. As a believer serving in the kingdom while working in a secular or other employment, I enjoin you to avoid the temptation to monetize your service to God. What can a person give in exchange for their soul? Were God to require payment from you for what He has done and does for you, where would you be? Forever and irremediably lost.

Churches suffer because believers require payment to serve. Churches also suffer because believers refuse to serve, thus compelling the church to pay others for work that members should do as their service to God. The standard statement has now become, 'Why not hire professionals to do it?' But it does not include, 'I will pay for the hiring of those professionals.' We neither pay nor do.

As you advance in your walk with the Lord, I say to you, 'Pay and do.' Do what you can, and contribute financially so your local church can pay people to do what none of you can. Learn skills that will be useful for your church as part of your service to God. Do not only put money in the offering; put some sweat in as well.

You will face challenges as you serve God. There will be opposition from within and without. Carnal people in the church, the devil, and even your own weaknesses will conspire to discourage you and endeavour to demobilise you. Stay engaged. All the heroes of the faith dealt with opposition. Paul gives a telling account of the woes he faced in the course of service – beatings, shipwreck, hunger, etc. – and he stood firm. His letters show the pain of betrayal, and the joy of fellowship with like-minded devoted workers for God. Through it all, he never wavered, stating that he served the Lord 'with great humility and with tears, although I was severely tested by the plots of the Jews' (Acts 20.19).

Resilience

Serving God calls for resilience. Pray for resilience. Resilience is a fruit of strength and of commitment. Make up your mind that you are called to share the burden, not simply partake of the benefits. Commit, grow, and keep going. Love the church with passion; love the work of God with passion. That was one of Paul's secrets. He truly loved the church, he loved God, and he believed in the power of the gospel.

Faith

Believe in the power of the gospel to change lives and to change the world. Believe that Jesus is building the church and that the gates of hell cannot prevail against it. It will energise you as you serve.

You are part of a winning team. Use God's Word to fight discouragement. Remember, you are on the Lord's team. Since He believes in the work, so much that He gave up the glories of heaven to suffer the ignominy of becoming human and dying at the hands of sinful creation, then you should also believe in it and do it with zeal and faith.

There is so much more that can be said about our attitude as we serve our Lord, but the space of this little book will not permit further development. Bear in mind that you are neither spectator nor client; you are the one who serves in humility. Your labour in the Lord is not in vain and God rewards those who are faithful.

REWARDS OF SERVICE

In serving God, we are doing that which is our responsibility. We should not be expecting special commendation, yet God still chooses of His own volition to reward those who are faithful. We are not more honourable than God. Whether we seek it or not, He always rewards those who honour Him.

Before we were of any use to Him in kingdom service, He gave us the greatest gift He had, Jesus. No man is ever worse off serving God than not serving God. In fact, we are distinctly better off, in every respect. To serve God is to obey, to obey is to be blessed. Let me give you a quick foretaste of some of the benefits of serving God.

Joy

For me, the greatest reward for serving God is having the honour of contributing to the joy of God in seeing His desires become a manifest reality in the earth. Close on its heels is my own joy in seeing God's will performed in the lives of individuals, and in His church. Every victory fills me with great gladness. Every healing, salvation, deliverance, etc. makes my heart sing. We share in God's joy when we serve Him and see His work advance. That is a joy that I pray you will experience continually in your life. It overwhelms the adverse circumstances of life.

Divine favour

Divine favour is another benefit of kingdom service. Psalm 101 speaks in verse six of the favour granted the faithful of the land. To be faithful is to be faithful not only in profession, but in lifestyle, in obedience to God. Think of the favour granted to Anna, a woman who had served God faithfully for eighty four years since the death of her husband. She was one of the priviledged few to whom God revealed the identity of the baby Jesus when he was brought to the temple. The same obtains for Simeon, a man called righteous and devout. What a great favour of God to have been told specifically by the Lord that he would not die until he had seen the Messiah.[2]

Many in their generation would not even recognize the miracle worker and great teacher as the Messiah, they were spiritually blind. And to these ones, God granted the astounding favour of seeing a child and recognizing the Messiah. They were friends of God and received special treatment because of their commitment and service to God. Where men are crying out in confusion, you will be enjoying the favour of God and revelation and understanding.

There are many such instances of God's special favour coming upon His choice servants in Scripture, in diverse areas. Choose to be one of those.

Honour

Honour from God has been promised to kingdom servants. Jesus said concerning those who serve and follow Him, 'where I am, my servant also will be.' And that place is a place of honour. This will thrill you; the verse contin-

---

[2]. Luke 2.22-36

ues by saying this: *'My Father will honour the one who serves me'* (John 12:26). So there is a present reward and also an eternal reward in the presence of the Father.

Divine provision

Paul the Apostle wrote in that beautiful letter to the church in Philippi (often called the most joyful letter in the New Testament) about God's provision for all their needs. It is a favourite of those asking God for money or material blessings. The church in Philippi had been a strong supporter of the ministry of God through Paul. They had served, they had given very generously, and they had taken their part in the work of the kingdom.

Paul, thoroughly moved by their dedication to the kingdom, was inspired by the Holy Spirit to give God's response to their labour, and it is this: that He would supply all their needs in ways commensurate with His own glory. That is huge. In the next chapter on giving, we will deal in greater detail with the matter of provision. For now, know that precedent and promise in the Word of God agree that when you serve God, He will more than take care of your material needs.

Remarkable occurrences

Remarkable occurrences have been the lot of many in Scripture who served God. One woman, the Shunamite woman, provided accommodation and nourishment for one of God's prophets, Elisha. As a result, God gave her a child. The child at some point fell ill and died, but through the prophet's prayers, he was brought back to life. It is worth noting that the woman was selfless in her giving; she expected nothing in return. When the man of God prodded her to say what she wanted, she presented no request. It was his idea, on hearing from his servant that she was childless to tell her God would give her a child. It is possible to serve God so selflessly that He will stir the heart of a person to meet a need in our lives and intercede for us in time of difficulty.

Return on investment

Whatever you can think or accept to do for God, God can and will do much more for you. That is the principle Jesus enunciated when His disciples wanted to know where they stood since they had left everything to follow Him. This came after one wealthy individual had declined to give up his posessions to follow Jesus. Jesus said to His disciples:

> 'Truly I tell you,' Jesus replied, '"no one who has left home or brothers or sisters or mother or father or children or fields for me and the gospel will fail to receive a hundred times as much in this present age (homes, brothers, sisters, mothers, children and fields – and with them, persecutions) and in the age to come, eternal life'" (Mark 10.29-30).

Jesus taught that what we do in service has a corresponding return. Those who serve God in giving will receive in return. Those who serve God in prayer and fasting and do it the right way will receive a reward. Then those who give up property, family, etc to follow Him will receive more of the same in this world, Mathew's gospel says 'many times more'; along with persecutions, and eternal life.

Serve God regardless of the circumstances. Remember the people in the time of the prophet Malachi. At some point they became discouraged. Some complained that it was futile to serve God, that they gained nothing from doing His will and that the arrogant were prospering. Sounds familiar doesn't it? Familiar but false. God's promise is that there is a difference between those who serve Him and those who do not.

> 'And you will again see the distinction between the righteous and the wicked, between those who serve God and those who do not ' (Malachi 3.18).

Paul the apostle served God under the most trying circumstances and He still reminded us that 'God is faithful, and will not forget your labour of love.' I pray that you have been further energised to dedicate your life to serving God, to give freely what you have received freely. I pray that, like Jesus in John 17.4, you are able to boldly say towards the end of your life that you have glorified God and have finished the work He gave you to do. Or that, like Paul, you will be able to say that you have run the race, you have finished the course and that a crown of righteousness now awaits you.

*

Scriptures for meditation

1 Corinthians 16.15-16 – 'You know that the household of Stephanas were the first converts in Achaia, and they have devoted themselves to the service of saints. I urge you, brothers, to submit to such as these, and to everyone who joins in the work and labours in it.'

John 12.26 – 'Whoever serves me must follow me; and where I am, my servant also will be. My Father will honour the one who serves me.'

Deuteronomy 13.4 – 'It is the LORD your God you must follow, and him you must revere. Keep his commands and obey him; serve him and hold fast to him.'

Matthew 6.20-21,24 – 'But store up for yourselves treasures in heaven, where moth and rust do not destroy and where thieves do not break in and steal. For where your treasure is, there your heart will be also. ... "No one can serve two masters. Either he will hate the one and love the other, or he will be devoted to the one and despise the other. You cannot serve both God and Money.'

Romans 12.11– "Neither be lacking in zeal , but keep your spiritual fervour, serving the Lord.'

1 Timothy 1.12 – 'I thank Christ Jesus our Lord, who has given me strength, that he considered me faithful, appointing me to his service.'

[See also Luke 17.7-10; Revelation 7.15; Deuteronomy 28.47-48]

*

Points to ponder

- Believe that Jesus is building the church and that the gates of hell cannot prevail against it. It will energise you as you serve.
- Intrinsic to God's purpose in saving us is that we would be reconciled to Him and that we would serve Him.
- When people truly understand redemption, they will be falling over themselves to make themselves useful to God.

Discussion questions

1. Explain what service to God is.
2. Why serve?
3. What is the attitude of the kingdom servant?
4. Does God reward service? How?

Prayer

Father, thank You for the work of service that Jesus accomplished on the earth for my sake.

Because of Him I am saved and reconciled with You. I commit my life to You for kingdom service. This is my purpose Lord, to fully accomplish every good work you prepared for me before the foundation of the world. Here I am Lord, send me and make my life one of glorious service to You. In Jesus' name, Amen.

8

Fast

The year is 1756. England is in a state of turmoil; the victory of the French in the seven-year war raises the spectre of an invasion by France. France, it is said, has built boats specially for the occasion. The nation is in fear. King George calls a national fast. Men such as John Wesley write copiously to rally Christians to participate. The fast is a huge success; the turnout is massive; John Wesley writes the following in his journals: *'Friday, February 6. The fast-day was a glorious day; such as London has scarce seen since the Restoration. Every church in the city was more than full, and a solemn seriousness sat on every face. Surely God heareth the prayer; and there will yet be 'a lengthening of our tranquillity'.*

And lengthening there was. The French fleet is sunk in part, the remainder flees, and the impending invasion is thwarted. To Christians, the victory is God's response to a nation that humbled itself before God. A day of thanksgiving is set aside. Charles Wesley wrote several songs of thanksgiving, one is 'The Song of Moses'. Stanzas three to five read:

> The Lord, he is a man of war,
> In every age the same;
> Let Britain saved with shouts declare
> The great Jehovah's name:
> Jehovah on our foes did frown
> Amidst their furious boast,
> And cast their chosen captains down,
> And drowned half their host.

> Into the depths they sunk as lead,
> Who thee and thine opposed,
> They sunk at once; and o'er their head
> The mighty waters closed!
> Thine own right hand with power supreme,
> With glorious dreadful power,
> In pieces dashed their ships and them,
> And bade the gulf devour
>   In vain the fierce invader swore,
> "I will lay waste their isle,
> Pursue them on their native shore,
> And seize, and part the spoil;
> Will on the heretics abhorred
> My lust of vengeance cloy,
> And draw my consecrated sword,
> And young and old destroy."
>   For great in majesty divine,
> Thy wrathful Spirit blew,
> Blasted their arrogant design,
> And all their host o'erthrew:
> Into the depths they sunk as lead
> Who thee and thine opposed,
> They sunk at once; and o'er their head
> The mighty waters closed.

The sense of victory is palpable in these verses. The confidence that it was wrought by God as a consequence of prayer and fasting is obvious. From time immemorial, humans have understood the vital nature of fasting coupled with prayer in enhancing spiritual life and attaining victories. Fasting is a desirable spiritual discipline for every believer to acquire from the beginning of their walk, a vital pointer for winning the prize at the end of the Christian race. So what is fasting? Why fast? When should we fast? How do we fast? Finally, what are the consequences of fasting?

WHAT IS FASTING?

Fasting is denying oneself of natural pleasures, foregoing food for a season to gain some spiritual benefit.

Fasting, as a practice, is common to many religious traditions. Men have always known that denying the appetites of the body procured spiritual advantage. It is an ancient practice in Christianity that seems to have fallen on hard times in our present age. The Scriptures record many fasts, corporate and individual, that were the means for a radical turnaround and forward motion in the circumstances of a person or nation.

Samuel, the prophet, called the nation of Israel to a corporate fast, as did Jehoshaphat the king, Nehemiah the governor, Ezra to the group with him, the prophets and teachers at Antioch, and the king of Nineveh his own people. Individuals like Moses, David, Nehemiah, Paul, Daniel, Anna the prophetess, and our Lord are recorded as fasting. Before Jesus left the earth, He made it clear that His disciples would fast on His departure by teaching on the right attitude to have 'when you fast'. When He, the bridegroom, was taken away, He said His people would fast.

And fast they did. Fasting was embraced by the early church. In the first few centuries of the church, it was customary to fast twice a week, Wednesdays and Fridays; interestingly, fasting was generally prohibited on Sundays as it was the day of the resurrection of the Lord and was considered a day of celebration. Gradually, the Lenten fast was introduced as well. The writings of the church Fathers extolled the virtues of fasting. Saint Augustine considered, in a sermon titled 'On Prayer and Fasting' that, 'Fasting cleanses the soul, raises the mind, subjects one's flesh to the spirit, renders the heart contrite and humble, scatters the clouds of concupiscence, quenches the fire of lust, and kindles the true light of chastity'. Many went into various extremes. Others abandoned the practice altogether in the course of the history of the church. In order to fast appropriately, a biblical approach is required.

There are varying forms of fasts. For instance, there is the partial fast such as Daniel did, which some call the Daniel fast, where an individual abstains from meat and rich foods, feeding only on vegetables and water. There is the total fast, abstaining from all foods and drinking only water. There is also the Esther fast, a fast called at a crucial time in the history of God's people when they were under threat of extermination by the Persian king. Queen Esther asked the Jews to fast for three days and nights, abstaining from food and from water. Water is essential for life and it is not advised to go beyond three days without water. Humans can abstain from food for longer periods than they can from water before starvation sets in.

How long should one fast? Fasting durations can vary from 6am to 6pm, 24 hours, 48 hours, 3 days, 7 days, 21 days, or 40 days. On the longer fasts, you may break in the evenings at 6pm, so that will be one meal a day, or fast all the way through, eating only at the end of the fast. Initially, it is advisable to start with short fasts and build up from there. Bear in mind that purpose is essential to fasting, and direction from the Holy Spirit is crucial in determining the kind and duration of a fast. Seek counsel from godly, wise leaders as you begin your journey into a life of regular fasting.

WHY FAST?

When we fast, we express our need for God and for His assistance, we express our dependence on Him, and we demonstrate our commitment to achieving the desired objective. In fasting, we deny the flesh to become more spiritually sensitive and more able to hear God and seize our victory.

Repentance and mourning

In the Bible there are several instances of individuals or groups fasting as a sign of repentance or in mourning over a particular sin or situation. For instance, David fasted when judgement was pronounced over his sin of adultery and murder in the matter of Uriah and his wife Bathsheba, whom David took unlawfully. Ahab also repented, wore sackcloth, fasted, and walked around utterly dejected. He was arguably the most evil ruler Israel had ever known. Before you pronounce yourself free of such shenanigans, consider the case of Nehemiah and Daniel. They fasted and repented over the sins of their people, for whom the nation had been sent into exile and was sorely disgraced and humbled. They mourned and their prayers are instructive as to the manner in which we approach God in similar situations. They acknowledged their sin and the sin of their people, recognised God's greatness and His right to punish them for their wrongdoing, and implored His mercy.

Even the heathen got in on the act. Remember Jonah? Jonah was a rebellious prophet who was sent by God to warn the city of Nineveh of impending judgement because of their nefarious ways. Jonah tried to avoid the mission by running away, but God caught up with him and in dire straits, the prophet finally capitulated and resolved to go to Nineveh. He walked the streets of the city warning the people of judgement. On hearing this, they promptly went into mourning before God. The king decreed a fast of mourning and repentance, imploring the mercy of God, and they were spared. Jonah was none too pleased because that was precisely why he sought to flee the assignment; he knew the mercy of God would prevail if the people repented.

Why does this matter? Well, it is quite remarkable that for many believers in this generation, repentance is an alien concept. In essence, we no longer acknowledge wrongdoing. We simply chafe at the pain our wrongdoing has occasioned. For us, the experience of pain seems to vitiate culpability. People commit the most egregious sins and proceed to speak publicly about their trials, and make triumphant assertions of how they made it through, all without the slightest hint of brokenness over their wrongdoing or repentance for flouting the law of God. Then they add insult to injury by turning their evildoing into an occasion for gain as they tour the conference circuit, picking up fat cheques for 'telling their story'. For greater effect, it will include a sombre period of questioning God and wondering where He was when they were 'going through their stuff', that stuff being the fallout of their sin. Churches and religious organisations are not exempt.

Be quick to repent. Consider God superior to yourself. When you are bearing the brunt of your own unrighteous behaviour, do not pose as a victim. Accept that you failed God. That is the key to true restoration. Those who have freely received forgiveness and grace in Christ should be the most tender-hearted and sensitive where sin is concerned. Fasting is not indispensable to repentance, but it will not hurt in expressing your commitment and renewed consecration. There is a place, even today, to do as Daniel and Nehemiah did, for the church as a body to fast and repent for the sins of the nation.

A humbling of oneself

To fast is to humble ourselves before God. The psalmist in Psalm 25 speaks of fasting on behalf of an afflicted friend. In fasting, he humbled his soul before the Lord. Ahab, a particularly evil king of Israel, when threatened with judgement is also said to have 'humbled himself' in fasting. And because he humbled himself, judgement was averted.

Whatever the cause of the fast, whatever the circumstance, taking part in a fast is expressing humility before God. It is expressing subservience to and dependence on God. You make yourself vulnerable before Him to seek His attention and assistance. You acknowledge His superiority over yourself.

A desperate cry for help in time of trouble

There is a fast that is a desperate cry out to God for immediate assistance in a time of great distress and need. Such was the case of Jehoshaphat and the nation of Israel when faced with mighty armies in coalition against them. They were puny and insignificant and desperately needed divine intervention. Jehoshaphat mobilised the entire nation to fast and pray and seek the Lord, and God responded by granting him the victory.

Such indeed was the case of Ezra, who, on preparing to leave the courts of Babylon to return with a group of exiles to Judah, had boasted of the might and goodness of his God. He thus found himself unable to turn to the king for protection from the perils of the route. In desperation, cognisant of grave danger without divine intervention, he and the people with him fasted and prayed. God heard them and gave them safe passage.

Daniel did more than mourn. He ended his prayer crying out to God to move, to act on behalf of His people. Nehemiah cried for help. He asked that God would grant him favour with the king as he had a request to make for the good of God's people.

A child of God need not go through life in fear of danger of potential problems. When difficulties arise, we must arise and seek the Lord in prayer and fasting. In ministry, we cannot be prescriptive, but many of the problems people face and for which they want hands laid on them can be dealt with by themselves if they will take the time to wait on God in prayer and fasting. He will bring deliverance and victory.

A trigger of revelation

Akin to the cry of distress is fasting that triggers revelation and the attendant breakthrough. When Jehoshaphat and his army fasted, God gave them a revelation through a prophet. The prophet told them exactly what they needed to do and how the Lord would give them the victory. They obeyed to the letter and the hand of the Lord prevailed against their enemies. Sometimes all we need is to know what to do, and that information is often conveyed as we fast and wait on the Lord.

Sometimes, when we face longstanding problems, there may be vicious enemies resisting us. It is useful to engage in fasting and prayer to get insight from God as to the particular problem and potential solution. I once heard a pastor tell the story of a woman in his church whose child went from being an A student to the back of the class. She had prayed, but nothing was happening; she embarked on a seven-day fast and at the end of the fast, the Lord gave her a dream that showed the origin of the problem. She confronted the problem head on and instantly the boy's performance was back to normal.

Cornelius was a man much given to fasting, prayer, and giving of alms. He was also the first Gentile to receive the gospel from the Apostles. It was as he fasted and waited on the Lord that an angel of the Lord appeared to him, to instruct him to send for Peter and receive the truth about Christ. The consequence of this was that the Gentiles received the baptism of the Holy Spirit and the church was forever changed.

Remember Anne, who for 84 years had dedicated her life to God. She served God in the temple night and day, the Bible tells us, by fasting and prayer. She also received revelation of the identity of Jesus and was on hand to welcome the baby when He was brought to the temple for dedication by His parents.

When you desperately need guidance for a breakthrough in your life, don't hesitate to take some time to fast and pray if you feel the Holy Spirit is directing you to do so. It helps to block out other voices and focus on God. He is faithful to grant understanding to those who desire it. He will show the spiritual forces resisting your advancement.

> *Consider God superior to yourself. When you are bearing the brunt of your own unrighteous behaviour, do not pose as a victim. Accept that you failed God.*

Spiritual sensitivity, cleansing, and power

There is no doubt that when we have taken time out to fast and wait on the Lord in prayer, our spiritual sensitivity is heightened and our flesh quieted. We are less subject to physical cravings or mental distractions. Our spirit man is more dominant, thus flowing with the Holy Spirit comes more easily. It is as if you were released from a cage. Physical weakness notwithstanding, there is an unselfconsciousness and a greater God consciousness in prayer than before. Spiritual things captivate us more than previously and God's Word is fresher to our taste. Our spiritual appetites are heightened as our physical ones are denied. This greater spiritual sensitivity translates into greater harmony with God, revelation, and a heightened manifestation of the gifts of the Spirit. We are also often blessed with greater demonstrations of the power of the Holy Spirit.

We see this in our own local church in monthly, three-day prayer and fasting sessions. We have seen deep cleansing from sin, the people are spiritually stronger, and the power of God is present to set people free of demons and occult domination. In the short time that it has been ongoing, it has led to a radical change in the lives of the people and in the church as a whole. As a result of strong teaching and consistent fasting and prayer, we are witnessing a consistent stream of miracles. Deliverance from evil spirits is a manifestation of the power of God and persons involved in deliverance testify to the effectiveness of prayer and fasting. Any minister who wants to move in the power of God will find that periods of fasting will be of great use in fine tuning them and releasing God's power in their lives.

One great general in the history of Christianity in Nigeria was Joseph Ayo Babalola, who was among the founders of the still buoyant Christ Apostolic Church. He had a strong belief in the effectiveness of prayer and fasting. It was after a seven-day fast that he received the mandate to ministry with a divine visitation. Even after this, he knew he still lacked the power to minister and went on several fasts after which he was endued with power. Babalola was instrumental in the revival of the 1930s in Southern

Nigeria. Through his ministry, many turned from animism to Christ, burning their fetishes and idols. He defied the interdiction on entering magic forests and survived unharmed by evil spirits. He had a powerful healing and deliverance ministry. He was used by God to change Southern Nigeria radically with the Gospel. Christianity was no longer a white man's religion practised alongside idol worship. It became known as a religion for all men, as Christ was for all men, one of power, greater than those of local idols. He was known for his life of prayer and fasting.

Ministry direction

Fasting makes us receptive to spiritual direction in ministry and leadership. The Apostle Paul is arguably the greatest Christian who ever lived. His release to ministry came about as a result of fasting and prayer. In Acts 13.2, as the leadership of the Antioch church ministered to the Lord and fasted, the Holy Spirit spoke to them. He asked them to set apart Paul and Barnabas for the ministry He had called them to. They obeyed and so began the greatest evangelistic ministry in the New Testament and in the history of the church.

Paul was himself a fasting man and many a time he had to change his plans because of directions received from the Holy Spirit. Once he tried to go to Bithynia and the Holy Spirit prevented him. He received direction to go to Macedonia when he had not intended to do so, and he went. He was prevented from going to Asia when he had planned to go. This contributed to the success of his life, such that he was confident as he neared the end of his life that he had run his race as he ought and that he would now receive his crown. I pray that you also are able to face death with the same assurance, I enjoin you to live a life of consistent fasting and praying before the Lord that you might win the prize.

One cannot overemphasise the importance of the spiritual discipline of fasting and keeping the flesh under subjection to the spirit. Jesus gave it His stamp of approval. At the same time, you will undoubtedly encounter many who do not fast. The modern church has grown flabby and content, but war rages while we feast.

HOW DO I FAST?

There are some fairly obvious things to keep in mind when you fast. These will enhance the effectiveness of your fast and ensure that you are doing more than skipping meals.

Prayer

Fasting should never be done alone without prayer, otherwise it becomes a mere diet. Follow the example of Daniel. Daniel was an exile in Babylon. Through his spiritual discipline and faithfulness to God, he rose to great prominence in the civil administration. He was a prophet and made a habit of fasting and praying regularly. When he fasted, he prayed with great passion and great intensity, as indicated by this passage: *'So I turned to the Lord God and pleaded with him in prayer and petition, in fasting, and in sackcloth and ashes' (Daniel 9.3)*.

There are three power ingredients in this verse: prayer (including petition), fasting, and repentance.

Humility and secrecy

Jesus taught that fasting should be done in secret and in an attitude of humility. You may be compelled to tell those close to you (at home, for instance), so they do not worry about you not eating, but you want to refrain from trumpeting it abroad. Don't look the part. It should be between your Father and yourself. It should not be a spiritual badge of honour, nor does it make you deserving of any special consideration. Jesus has this to say in Matthew 6.16-18:

> 'When you fast, do not look sombre as the hypocrites do, for they disfigure their faces to show men they are fasting. I tell you the truth, they have received their reward in full. But when you fast, put oil on your head and wash your face, so that it will not be obvious to men that you are fasting, but only to your Father, who is unseen; and your Father, who sees what is done in secret, will reward you.'

Do you see that God intends to reward you for fasting? That is a precious truth that should encourage you every time you fast. God promises you a reward, so don't lose it by publicising your fast. In the case of a corporate fast, there are several of you fasting together so the dynamics are somewhat altered, but the principles are the same – humility, discretion, no showing off towards those who are not fasting with you.

Time in the Word of God

Since the goal is to seek the Lord and derive some spiritual advancement from the fast, it is important to listen to God in His Word. Let's look at another example of a fast in God's Word. This time it is in the book of Nehemiah. We have talked about the fact that Nehemiah himself fasted before going to ask for favour from the king. But here, all the people assembled under the leadership of Nehemiah and Ezra, the priest, and they all fasted. Note the particular attention paid to the Word of God:

> 'On the twenty-fourth day of the same month, the Israelites gathered together, fasting and wearing sackcloth and having dust on their heads. Those of Israelite descent had separated themselves from all foreigners. They stood in their places and confessed their sins and the wickedness of their fathers. They stood where they were and read from the Book of the Law of the Lord their God for a quarter of the day, and spent another quarter in confession and in worshipping the Lord their God' (Nehemiah 9.1-3).

The ingredients here are fasting, repentance, confession, reading of God's Word, and worship – which is a form of prayer. Imitate these and you will do very well indeed.

Focus and faith

Be focused. There is a firmness of purpose required to get results from fasting. You have an objective. Do not take no for an answer. Pursue it firmly as you fast and pray. Don't be distracted to pray about everything under the sun. When you read the prayers of the people who fasted in the Bible, they were pursuing one objective and obtained it.

You must also believe that you will achieve your desired end. It is called faith. God has promised to hear and answer, so hold Him to His Word and stay firm and dogged till the answer comes. Sometimes the answer comes faster than you imagined. Once, I was seeking direction about moving after my school year came to an end. I was very keen to leave Europe and move back home. Someone said to me in passing, 'Why don't you pray about it?' I realised I was about to make a major life decision based solely on my emotions, so I undertook a one-week fast. On the very first day, God spoke very clearly in my heart that I was to stay in France. I agreed, but struggled with life in France for several years. Today, I lead a ministry that is touching over a hundred nations from my base in Paris, having ministered exclusively in French for the past eight years.

I also pastor a local, French-speaking church. God's ways are not ours. In fasting and praying, His will is laid out for us clearly so we do not miss our way.

Do Isaiah 58

Let me tell you the story. The people were puzzled. They appeared to be very sincere, they 'seemed eager' to know God and to obey Him (as many of us appear to onlookers), and they prayed daily. They were fasting assiduously but getting no results from their fasting. So they began to complain to God that their fasting was not yielding fruit; God apparently was not paying them any attention, and they insisted on knowing why. Sounds very familiar to me. In response, God calls the prophet to thunder in their ears and raise his voice like a trumpet to inform this 'rebellious' people of what they were doing wrong that was rendering their fasting and praying ineffective. The problem is that while they fasted, they also indulged in the following:

- selfish behaviour
- exploitation of their workers (or anyone else)
- contention, quarrels, and strife
- physical violence

He said you cannot do such things and expect your prayer to be heard on high. Need I say more? What pleases God is this:

- relieving injustice and oppression
- generosity
- care for the needy
- provision for one's own family
- absence of maliciousness and evil
- right treatment of people

For this, God promises some very rich rewards. He truly is a rewarder of the righteous. Read Isaiah 58 and enjoy the rich rewards He promises. Fasting is of the heart and of the body. We fast from food and bad behaviour. When the King of Nineveh heard the threats of destruction against his city from Jonah, he sent out an edict to his people that they were to fast and give up their evil conduct and abstain from violence. Their repentance was so profound that God heard and forgave them. Nineveh was saved.

There is so much that can be said about the benefits of fasting. Bear in mind that no one seeks God in vain. When we think we are doing things right and we still do not hear from God, we must be doing something wrong. As He showed Israel in Isaiah 58, He will always show us.

Conclusion

> 'But those who hope in the Lord will renew their strength. They will soar on wings as eagles; they will run and not grow weary, they will walk, and not be faint' (Isaiah 40.31).

When we fast, we gain new strength, spiritual sensitivity and power, direction from heaven, victory over the flesh, victory over sin and temptation, the rewards of obedience, answers to prayer, and divine breakthroughs like Cornelius.

*

Scriptures for meditation

Matthew 6.16-18 – 'When you fast, do not look sombre as the hypocrites do, for they disfigure their faces to show men they are fasting. I tell you the truth, they have received their reward in full. But when you fast, put oil on your head and wash your face, so that it will not be obvious to men that you are fasting, but only to your Father, who is unseen; and your Father, who sees what is done in secret, will reward you.'

Daniel 10.3 – 'I ate no choice food; no meat or wine touched my lips; and I used no lotions at all until the three weeks were over.'

Nehemiah 1.4 – 'When I heard these things I sat down and wept. For some days I mourned and fasted and prayed before the God of heaven.'

Nehemiah 9.1-3 – 'On the twenty-fourth day of the same month, the Israelites gathered together, fasting and wearing sackcloth and having dust on their heads. Those of Israelite descent had separated themselves from all foreigners. They stood in their places and confessed their sins and the wickedness of their fathers.'

Jonah 3.5-6 – 'The Ninevites believed God. They declared a fast, and all of them, from the greatest to the least, put on sackcloth. When the news reached the king of Nineveh, he rose from his throne, took off his royal robes, covered himself with sackcloth and sat down in the dust.'

Daniel 9. 3 – 'So I turned to the Lord God and pleaded with him in prayer and petition, in fasting and in sackcloth and ashes.'

*

Points to ponder

- Fasting is a desirable spiritual discipline for every believer to acquire from the beginning of their walk.
- In fasting, we deny the flesh to become more spiritually sensitive and more able to hear God and seize our victory.
- When you read the prayers of the people who fasted in the Bible, they were pursuing one objective and obtained it.

Discussion questions

1. What is fasting?
2. Why fast?
3. What do you do during a fast?
4. Explain some of the benefits of fasting.

Prayer

Father, thank You for the grace to fast.

I commit to making this valuable spiritual discipline an intrinsic part of my life. Make me sensitive to your voice so I know when to fast and thus miss no opportunity to fast and pray. I believe that as I fast, all your plans for me will become manifest reality. In Jesus' name, Amen!

9

Give

> "How you handle money reveals volumes about your priorities, loyalties and affections. In fact, it directly dictates many of the blessings you will (or won't) experience in life."
>
> Robert Morris
> (The Blessed Life)

'Command those who are rich in this present world not to be arrogant nor to put their hope in wealth, which is so uncertain, but to put their hope in God, who richly provides us with everything for our enjoyment. Command them to do good, to be rich in good deeds, and to be generous and willing to share. In this way they will lay up treasure for themselves as a firm foundation for the coming age, so that they may take hold of the life that is truly life' (1 Timothy 6.17-19).

The big supermarket in the shopping centre next to my house was closed one summer. What did I miss the most? Easy: roasted salted almonds, a UK import that I have seen nowhere else in Paris. These almonds are a treat. So much so that Nelson, my then 6-year-old nephew could hardly keep his hands off them the first time he tasted them. With the first mouthful, he turned to his father, 'Papa, have some. They are so delicious,' pressing him to share the goodness he had just savoured. I love watching them. They are unusually close. As a younger child, Nelson seemed to possess a most accurate 'Papa sensor'. Were 'Papa' to try to slip out of a room while Nelson's back was turned, Nelson would spin around, drop everything, cry 'Papa', and pursue.

Even today, take Nelson to the stores, buy him some article, and instinctively, he will turn to 'Papa' and say thank you. Of course, on gentle prodding, he will eventually acknowledge and thank the real buyer, but you suspect he still thinks his father had something to do with it.

Nelson wants to grow up and do what 'Papa' does. Nelson will have ice cream for dessert if 'Papa' is having it, otherwise he will pass. Nelson is enjoying some food ... does 'Papa' want some of it? He will gladly share, because in Nelson's world good comes from 'Papa.' 'Papa' is the author and source of all, and 'Papa' can have whatever he wants.

That is the best way I have found to describe to you the biblical perspective of the relationship between you, God, and money or any other material possessions you currently may own. Money and the usage thereof features prominently in the Scriptures and is an accurate reflection of spiritual understanding and maturity. As God is the source of all, securing that crown at the end of our lives will require that we align our financial and material lives with His Word and will. We receive from him, give to Him, and use money as He desires, knowing that He is the source of all our own. Let's delve deeper into this; let's look at three fundamental concepts that will shape our thinking in this area.

GOD AND MONEY

God claims ownership of everything

It is God's claim that all monetary resources on the earth are His possession, irrespective of the human hands in which they now reside. He made this somewhat unexpected – albeit perfectly logical – assertion at a time when His people, after returning from captivity, were trying to build a new temple. The glorious old one built by Solomon had suffered destruction in the hands of the Babylonians. Although Cyrus had sent them back to build the temple, providing supplies and support, they had faced much opposition. The work had stalled, and the people had grown despondent.

Earlier, when the foundations had been laid, the elders who had known the former temple wept as this new temple paled in comparison. But what could they do? They were former exiles, lacking the financial wherewithal or political independence to pull off an architectural feat. They were a people still for the most part in captivity. Their days of glory were long gone.

In the midst of this, God spoke to Haggai the prophet and acknowledged that the temple did not look like much, but they were not to worry. He was still with them. He was unimpressed by their financial wretchedness. In fact, as far as He was concerned, it was not an issue. At that point, the prophet makes this astounding declaration:

> 'The silver is mine and the gold is mine,' declares the LORD Almighty' (Haggai 2.8).

It is well within His powers to cause other nations to bring in the supply required.

From these circumstances so unlike our own comes a divine statement that radically alters our perspective. Do you see what God is saying here? He affirms Himself the rightful possessor of all the finances in the earth and of all the treasures of the world. Let me put it another way: all earthly wealth legitimately belongs to God and derives from God, irrespective of how the wealth is brought into the earth and in whose hands it is. Wealth – like everything else that God has made provision for, (sex, marriage, intelligence, etc.) – can be perverted, illegally acquired, and wrongfully utilised. In spite of this, the divine ownership of wealth is not to be faulted or doubted. The implications are huge if we will dare to believe them.

All things and people are His

The Bible also states that the earth belongs to God and all that it contains, the entire world and all those who inhabit it. He is the rightful owner of every person on the earth and everything. They may hate Him, rebel against Him, but He owns them.

God willingly gives everything

He gives all things

Not only does God own, but He also gives. John 3.16 is perhaps the best known verse in the Bible and it talks about the giving nature of God. For God so loved the world that He *gave* His only Son that anyone who believed in Him should not perish but have eternal life. The shining example of God's giving nature is the giving of His Son; through this most perfect of gifts, eternal life is granted to undeserving sinners. The giving nature of God is often clouded by our ingratitude and greed due to the fall; now that we are redeemed, we must make it our ambition to value and savour it.

Furthermore, the Scriptures let us understand that, having given us His Son, there can be no doubt that God would give us everything else. A child of God must rest in the assurance that He has the full intention of ensuring provision for life – spiritual, mental, and material. We start a new life in Christ of entrusting our entire lives to God, all that we own or will own. God the giver is still giving. Nothing He gives now will break the bank, for it will never equal what He has already given. You can stop there and shout 'Halleluiah'. But I must not get too excited too soon.

Paul the Apostle, in one of his inspired letters to his son in the faith, Timothy, instructs him to command the wealthy members of the congregation to demonstrate humility and not put their hope in their money, as money was so notoriously unreliable. Rather, they are to put their hope in God, 'who richly provides us with everything for our enjoyment' (1 Timothy 6.17). Here again, we see that God is the One who provides for you, and that you must train yourself not to rely on what you have or be intimidated by what you do not have. Rather, trust God. We see also that God gives money for personal enjoyment, among other things. Do not rely on your money, but on God, who is the source of all wealth. I think that sums it up very nicely.

God gives humans the ability to create wealth

The Bible expressly states that God gives the capacity to create wealth. That is what He said to His people as they prepared to enter the promised land. You know how people can often change when their financial fortunes improve for the better. All of a sudden, they do not have time for old friends, they turn their noses up at erstwhile pursuits, and they become ungrateful and self important. There are some believers who, as soon as they became wealthy, stopped serving God actively, found every reason not to be in church, and thought themselves too important for Christian concerns. Does it make sense to take a blessing and then use it as an excuse to disrespect the source of the blessing?

In the eighth chapter of Deuteronomy, God warns His people not to forget Him when they become wealthy and established because He is the One who gives them the capacity to produce wealth. Material resources are necessary for life on the earth and God enables us to create these resources. Of course, humans are variously endowed; some are gifted with massive wealth creation capability, others with management, etc. The creation of wealth is not evil. What matters is the way it is done, what it is used for, and how it is regarded. Take time to think on Deuteronomy 8.18:

> 'remember the Lord your God, for it is he who gives you the ability to produce wealth, and so confirms his covenant, which he swore to your forefathers, as it is today.'

Even though God allows us to enjoy some of the substance we generate, the creation of wealth is for divine purposes and must not be perverted into a desire for personal glory in wealth ownership. It is this perversion that leads to many fierce denunciations of wealthy persons in the Scriptures because wealth accumulation had become a personal end and no longer a means to an end.

There are many wealthy people today who think they are too rich to believe in God, and that religion is for the poor and clueless. Once there was a very wealthy man who delighted greatly in his possessions. His focus was on his wealth, savings, and storage capacity only. He had perverted his capacity to create wealth. He was self-satisfied and had great plans for financial expansion. Unfortunately, the very night he was making these lofty plans, he died and had to give an account of his life to God. Jesus called him a fool, said his soul would be required of him, and used him as an object lesson for all those who had material goods aplenty but were spiritually bankrupt. Such people are *'not rich towards God'*. (Luke 12.21)

I do not want to be that fool. Jesus tells us how to avoid that. He said that we are to focus above all things on the kingdom of God and its righteousness, and then all the other things (food, clothing, life necessities) would be added to us. He further said that the Father knows we need those things, a concept that is both enlightening and reassuring.

God requires believers to emulate Him as givers

The believer has the responsibility to provide supply for others – their family, the work of God, fellow believers in need, and the poor in general. This is a recurrent theme in God's Word. In the Old Testament, farmers were required by law to not harvest all of their grain, but to deliberately leave some behind for the poor and the alien who would come and gather for themselves. Psalm after psalm lauds generosity and giving.

In the New Testament, John the Baptist exhorted the people to generosity, to sharing their possessions, and warned them against extortion and dishonesty. Jesus spoke extensively about money and the use of money. He celebrated generous giving. He encouraged lending, total dependence on God, and giving Him priority before the pursuit of material needs. He warned strenuously against greed, against the pursuit of wealth that stifles God's

Word, and spoke of the impossibility of serving both God and money.

Everyone has to make a choice who his master will be. If God is our Master, we will treat money as a servant, to be used to help people and glorify God; not as a master to be protected and worshipped. Proverbs 22.9 tells us, '*A generous man will himself be blessed.*' This is a fundamental pointer to successful Christian living: learning to be generous and to give extravagantly. That is what God did from time immemorial; that is what He did in Jesus and that is what He is doing still in and for us today – giving extravagantly. God delights in generous people. Proverbs 22.9 very succinctly states that the generous person will be blessed. Jesus also talked about the rewards of giving. Since God is more generous than us, we cannot give more than He does. The more we give, the more we receive. Jesus said, 'Give, and it will be given to you' (Luke 6.38) – not the same thing that is given, but more. It will be pressed down, shaken together, and running over. This is a foundational principle of generosity. There are more, and we shall take them in order. What, then, are the principles that underpin Christian generosity?

Wealth production and management God's way

Think about the following points:

Success

God enables us to generate material resources through work and investment. We must believe that He will inspire us and bless our endeavours with success. A child of God should not be desperate to become rich. Many people work so hard they lose their health and even their families. Proverbs 23.4-5 warns against wearing oneself out to get rich. We are enjoined to show restraint because riches are highly volatile:

> 'Cast but a glance at riches, and they are gone, for they will surely sprout wings and fly off to the sky like an eagle' (Proverbs 23.5).

Holiness

God is able to empower us to produce wealth in a manner commensurate with His holiness. Consequently, we must abstain from activities that violate His principles, such as illicit endeavours or employing crooked methods. The book of Proverbs contains many admonitions against dishonesty in business and work. For instance, Proverbs 11.1 condemns the use of dishonest scales as something the Lord abhors. Here are some financial and business practices God hates:

- love of money
- stinginess

- laziness
- ingratitude
- defrauding workers (cheating)
- theft
- non-repayment of loans – *'The wicked borrow and do not repay'* (Psalm 37.21).
- craving for wealth – *'No-one can serve two masters… You cannot serve both God and Money'* (Matthew 6.24).
- trusting in money (uncertain riches) – *'Command those who are rich in this present world not to be arrogant'* (1 Timothy 6.17).

The same God who teaches and enables us to prosper is the One who says not to love money and serve it. There is a healthy perspective of wealth that a believer can and should have.

Goodness

God is able to generate resources in a manner commensurate with His goodness, thus He requires us to treat workers and colleagues in a kind and godly manner, to pay their wages, and to care for them. Isaiah 58 enumerates God's blessings on those who treat their workers fairly. Leviticus 19.13 even says not to keep a hired hand's wages overnight till the next day. In other words, pay your workers quickly.

Diligence and Faithfulness

Some people enjoy reading the gospel accounts because of the stories, but Jesus did not tell stories to entertain. Rather, He told stories to teach the willing and mystify the hard-hearted; you fall into the category of the willing since you are reading this book. In Luke 19.11-27, in a story similar to the Parable of the Talents that we saw earlier, He tells of a nobleman going off to receive a kingdom who entrusted ten minas to his ten servants. They were instructed to do business until he returned. The first two were diligent and obtained a return on investment, ten and five minas respectively; the third one was perfidious and lazy. He hid the money and made no good use of it.

On the return of the Master, He met with his servants and each rendered account of tasks accomplished in His absence. The first two handed over the gain, but the last tried to justify his sloth by impugning the character of the Master. He was duly punished for his wickedness, his mina was given to the one with ten and the first two were rewarded with greater responsibility.

Diligence and faithfulness in money matters are a qualifier for greater grace. Luke 16.10 tells us the words of Jesus on this topic:

> 'Whoever can be trusted with very little can also be trusted with much, and whoever is dishonest with very little will also be dishonest with much.'

In case you are wondering, by the little, He meant money.

Charity

God empowers us to create wealth to advance His purposes on the earth, to provide resources for His work and His church. God employs humans to distribute wealth so those who are deprived will be cared for. Wealth generation must serve charitable purposes. 1 John 3.17 states very bluntly, 'If anyone has material possessions and sees his brother in need but has no pity on him, how can the love of God be in him?' The Bible exhorts us to make money through hard work and wise investment so we can share:

> 'He who has been stealing, must steal no longer, but must work, doing something useful with his own hands, that he may have something to share with those in need' (Ephesians 4.28).

PRINCIPLES OF CHRISTIAN GENEROSITY

Why give, how do you give, and to whom do you give? Finally, what are the benefits of giving?

Why We Give

Reason One – Divine Ownership

The matter of divine ownership is omnipresent in all areas of giving. It is the primary reason we give. God claims ownership of all goods and all wealth in the earth. As some of it is in our hands, He is perfectly entitled to require us to distribute it as He sees fit. Giving becomes natural when we truly understand that He owns everything in our hands, in our wallet, and in our accounts – whether they be current, savings, or investment.

There was one man in Scripture who understood this very well. His name was David. King David had wanted to build a temple for the worship of God and God said no. As there was too much blood on his hands, his son Solomon would do it. So David did the next best thing, he contributed a veritable fortune to the Temple-building project, and the leaders and people emulated him. He proceeded to utter a most stirring prayer recorded in First Chronicles 29. Despite his vast fortune, his overall successful kingship and the greatness of his person, he understood this one thing: he was only giving back what he had previously received from God. I want you to read these verses slowly and contemplatively, as they are life-changing:

> 'David praised the Lord in the presence of the whole assembly, saying, "Praise be to you, o LORD, God of our father Israel, from everlasting to everlasting. Yours, O LORD, is the greatness and the power and the glory and the majesty and the splendor, for everything in heaven and earth is yours. Yours, O LORD, is the kingdom; you are exalted as head over all. Wealth and honour come from you; you are the ruler of all things. In your hands are strength and power to exalt and give strength to all. Now, our God, we give you thanks, and praise your glorious name. But who am I, and

who are my people, that we should be able to give as generously as this? Everything comes from you, and we have given you only what comes from your hand. We are aliens and strangers in your sight, as were all our forefathers. Our days on earth are like a shadow, without hope. O LORD our God, as for all this abundance that we have provided for building you a temple for your Holy Name, it comes from your hand, and all of it belongs to you' (1 Chronicles 29.10-16).

Notice the first verse – everything in heaven and earth is God's, and just in case you are tempted to retort that the psalmist meant spiritual things only, verse 12 clarifies things in saying, 'wealth and honour come from you.' Verse 14 defines true giving by saying that everything comes from God and he has only given what comes from the hands of God. He re-emphasises it in verse 16 and specifies that the abundance they had provided for the building of the temple comes from God's hands and all of it belongs to God. Breathtaking!

Whatever you give – to God, for the building of His church, or to others – all comes from God's hands and belongs to God, not you. Paul writes to the Corinthian church, *'What do you have that you did not receive?' (1 Corinthians 4.7).* The very capacity to think, to work, to function is a gift from Him.

Reason Two – Human Stewardship

This feeds naturally into the next point of the whys of giving: that is stewardship. Although God is the rightful owner of all wealth, all things, and all persons in the earth, He does not own a bank. He does no wire transfers of money, nor does He administer finances directly on the earth. That task has been assigned to His caretakers in the earth. This is called stewardship. To begin with, as we know, He not only gives to mankind, but He also endows individuals with the capacity to acquire wealth to fulfil His covenant. He entrusts individuals with the task of distributing wealth so none will be lacking. Thus, as a believer, the portion of His wealth in your possession is a trust, meant to be utilised at the Master's direction. They are to be seen as earthly resources for kingdom purposes. We are caretakers whom He appoints to dispense the grace as He directs. This is a radical paradigm shift for all of us.

Take time to think it through. It will greatly change your perspective of money and free you from all emotional entanglements with money. It will also cause you to be more circumspect in your spending and more diligent in the management of wealth. Because, as a steward, your faithfulness will be assessed and is being assessed on a continual basis. First Corinthians 4.2 tells us, 'Now it is required that those who have been given a trust must prove faithful.'

Reason Three – Imitators of God

According to the Bible, believers are partakers in the divine nature. Something of God's nature has been communicated to us and we are now to think, talk, and act like God. One of the most obvious ways in which that reality is expressed is in giving. God's love is seen in His giving, and so is ours. We thus imitate God by loving and express love by giving. We are not Christ-like until we begin to give. We are not lovers until we begin to give. When we love, we seek the good of the other and we work for their good.

Reason Four – Love and Obedience

Jesus said that those who love Him will do what He says. The requirement to give shines brightly through the pages of Scripture. So we give because we obey God and we obey because we love Him. If it matters to God, then it matters to us. If it fulfils the purpose of our Father, then we will do it to honour Him. His honour, then, far surpasses the value of the money.

Not only do we love God, but we love people, we love the church, we love the recipients of our generosity, and our heart is connected to their need. The quality of our giving demonstrates the sincerity of our love. Paul wrote to the Corinthians about giving and said he wanted to test the sincerity of their love by comparing it with the earnestness of others. If we are not eager to give, then we are deficient in love. How about this?

> 'This is how we know what love is: Jesus Christ laid down his life for us. And we ought to lay down our lives for our brothers. If anyone has material possessions and sees his brother in need but has no pity on them, how can the love of God be in him? Dear children, let us not love with words or tongue, but with actions and in truth' (1 John 3.16-18).

Do you see? Love can only be seen in what we do for others just as the love of Jesus was seen in what He gave up for us, His own life. That is why the Apostle John was very vehement about this.

Reason Five – Provision for God's Work

God's pattern has always been to make provision for His work on the earth through His people. In the Old covenant, believers were required to bring very specific gifts and offerings to the place of worship for the service at the altar. The system of giving and tithing was fairly elaborate.

Abraham was the first one mentioned in Scripture as having given a tithe to a priest, Melchizedek, who is a type of Christ. According to the book of Hebrews, Melchizedek received the tithe on the earth, and Christ receives it in Heaven. It is not necessary to split hairs about whether or not a Christian should tithe. The only time Jesus directly spoke about it was to approve the practice and condemn the attitude. As He receives it in Heaven, the New Testament believer who has inherited a better covenant should seek to do even more that those under a lesser covenant. I encourage you to take the tithe (ten percent of income) as your lowest level of giving to God. Then seek to grow far beyond as you administer God's resources in your hands. Do not be like those who starve the church to stuff their own bellies.

At a point after God's people returned from captivity, they postponed work on rebuilding the temple and got busy building fine houses for themselves to live in. God showed His displeasure at this state of affairs through the prophet Haggai. He told them that they were not blessed, that despite their hard work, it was as if their money was going into a purse with holes in it. He said this was because they had put their welfare ahead of the needs of God's house. Consequently, they were suffering drought and deprivation. They were to focus on building God's house and as they did, a remarkable thing happened. God spoke to them and told them that as from the first day, the day the first stone was laid, the situation had changed. He would bless them.

What is the implication for us today? Many believers focus on their own lives and barely give a thought to the needs of their local church, to providing for the ministry of Christ in the earth today. We are consumer-driven individuals, not provision-oriented. Today, churches have infrastructure needs and outreach opportunities that require financial input; believers in the local church are responsible for ensuring that nothing is lacking. The work of God must be amply provided for.

Some Christians live in very nice homes when their church meets in a hovel. It is disgraceful. As you join a local church and receive spiritual sustenance from there, open wide your wallet and give generously. Contribute financially to ensure your church owns its own property, and it is debt-free. If your pastor is concerned about money because you do not give, he will not be able to give his best spiritually, so you are shooting yourself in the foot. Do not be one of those who put pennies in the offering in church and then go out to lunch to feast and spend generously on their bellies. Honour God with money.

Israelites in the Old Testament were also required to make ample provision for the sustenance of the priests out of their own income, so that the priests would not devote themselves to anything other than the service of God. The Apostle Paul reiterated the principle that those who preach the gospel should derive their livelihood from the gospel, consequently from the generosity of believers (1 Corinthians 9.14).

Reason Six – Antidote to Greed

Giving is a powerful antidote to greed. If you are tight-fisted and think giving is going to be like pulling teeth, give anyhow. Don't simply pray and leave it at that; start riotous giving. It is often an acquired taste, but as you persevere, you will begin to derive intense joy from it and you will be delivered from greed.

Reason Seven – Path to Provision

God wants to bless His people financially, and He does it by multiplying back to them what they give. Whatever you give will yield a return. Read slowly through these words of Jesus in Luke 6.38:

> 'Give, and it will be given to you. A good measure, pressed down, shaken together and running over, will be poured into your lap. For with the measure you use, it will be measured to you.'

We deduce the following from Jesus' words.

First, when you give, you receive in return – *'Give, and it will be given to you.'*

Second, what comes to you is more than what you give – *'Good measure, pressed down, shaken together and running over, will be poured into your lap.'*

Third, God uses people to give to you – '*will be poured into your lap*' some translations say 'shall men add unto your bosom' in the same way as He uses you to give to others.

Fourth, the return is proportionate to the investment – '*For with the measure you use, it will be measured to you.*'

Reason Eight – Giving Brings Praise to God

Do you know that there is more than one way to praise God? Of course you can praise Him by singing or speaking praises, but you can also praise Him by giving to people. Your giving stirs up so much gratitude in their hearts that they overflow with praises to God. That is the message the Apostle Paul communicated to the Corinthian church when explaining to them about giving to the saints in Jerusalem. This is what he had to say, inspired by the Holy Spirit. Not only were they meeting the needs of other believers, but others, Paul said, will praise God for their obedience and their generosity.

Through your giving, you can help people understand the goodness and generosity of God. You can help change their image of God. When they are in desperate need and are praying, and you step up and help due to the prompting of the Holy Spirit, you confirm in their hearts the fact that God answers prayer. Their faith is made stronger and their hearts overflow in thanksgiving to God. And God is pleased, for them, and with you. That is how powerful your giving can be.

Your giving also contributes to your church owning its own building, which enables it to conduct programmes and activities that bring multitudes of people into the kingdom. All those people praise God, and your giving has contributed to that.

> *As you join a local church and receive spiritual sustenance from there, open wide your wallet and give generously.*

How We Give

Surrender

Give yourself wholly to God first. Paul the Apostle speaks of the astounding generosity of the Macedonians towards the believers in Jerusalem. The Macedonians, he said, first gave themselves wholly to God and then they gave in the collection for their brethren. Herein lies the first 'how' of giving: recognise His authority and ownership of you and be willing to relinquish earthly possessions to Him.

Receiving Divine Assistance

God helps us to do His will and we need His help. In the matter of giving, there are three primary, non-exhaustive things each of us can probably identify with as areas of need.

First, God will give us the right heart if we ask Him. He will, by His Spirit and through His Word, change our hearts. He will help us to want to give. The Bible says that He enables us to will and to do according to His good pleasure. Generosity pleases Him, so He will enable us to will in this matter too ... and why not? When I first came to be taught about tithing and giving, I struggled with it because I did not have a good understanding of it; it was alien to my thinking. But God enabled me to will, and to do. It is simply a matter of asking and obeying.

Secondly, He will give us seed to sow. Now if you are wondering what that means, know that giving is often referred to as 'sowing seed' in the Scriptures. Remember the principle of return? It is called sowing and reaping. In fact, every action is a seed that will generate a harvest of the same type. If you sow wickedness, you reap wickedness; if you sow love, you reap love. Giving is sowing. But to sow, you must have something to sow. Well, there is a guarantee from God's Word that He gives seed to the sower and that He will 'increase the store of seed' (2 Corinthians 9.10). If you have nothing to give, ask God to give you seed, and He will. And when He does, give it, don't eat it. In fact, why not make a habit of asking God when you receive any material thing to show you which is the seed and which is bread?

He will also give us wisdom to administer His resources in our hands. He will show us what to give and to whom.

He will put things in our hearts that we would not have thought of on our own. He will lay people on our hearts to give to that we do not even know are going through hard times. He will inspire us to be major sponsors of the Gospel.

So how do we give? We give by continually praying for and receiving help where needed – the right heart, the appropriate seed, the wisdom to administer and give in the right place to the right people.

Obedience

This ties in with the end of the previous paragraph. God will often direct us to give in a particular manner. It is imperative that we obey. We also give in obedience to His written Word, in the tithe and free offerings, in helping the poor, assisting our own families, etc.

Discretion

Jesus enjoined us to give discreetly without drawing attention to ourselves. He said that your right hand must not know what your left hand is doing; only Your Father in heaven will know. And He will reward you immeasurably. Wow!

Willingness/Cheerfulness

When God's people were in the wilderness, they began to build a tabernacle for the worship of God. They were all asked to contribute freely, and they did. It says that 'everyone who was willing and whose heart moved him came and brought an offering to the Lord for the work on the Tent of Meeting, for all its service and for the sacred garments (Exodus 35.21). Furthermore, when David made his aforementioned generous offering for the temple he was not allowed to build, the people also gave. We are told that that they rejoiced in giving. Giving should not be a sad, tug-of-war issue, as is often the case with believers. The people, we are told 'had given freely' and 'wholeheartedly' (1 Chronicles 29.9).

That is how we give, willingly and cheerfully. You see the importance of receiving divine assistance in our giving? Does it matter to God? Yes. Because God is not cash-strapped, it is our hearts that He is after. That is why we are told that God loves a cheerful giver. Many people will say if they are not feeling cheerful about giving, they will not give. Instead, we should commit to God that if we are not feeling cheerful about giving, we will work on the heart so that we will be able to give cheerfully. After all, as the psalmist puts it, *How can I repay the Lord for all his goodness to me? (Psalms 116.12).*

Generously

Don't just give, give much. Find opportunities to be generous and you will see God provide more and more for you so you can give more. The book of Proverbs says that *a generous person will prosper and whoever refreshes others will be refreshed* (Proverbs 11.25). Second Corinthians 9.6 gives us this promise:

> 'Remember this: Whoever sows sparingly will also reap sparingly, and whoever sows generously will also reap generously.'

Planned, spontaneously, in proportion to income

We learn from the first letter to the Corinthians that we give as God has blessed us. Each one is instructed to set aside some money on the first day of the week, in keeping with their income. We sometimes get carried away and empty our wallets, only to regret later. Therefore, as much as possible, plan your giving. Paul told the Corinthians to give as they had decided in their hearts. Seek God about your giving and plan as He leads you.

Planning should not preclude spontaneous, Spirit-led response to a crisis. There was a prophet called Agabus who went down to Antioch to prophesy that there would be a famine in Judea. The believers in Antioch promptly put together money to succour the saints in Jerusalem and sent the money via Paul and Barnabas.

Sacrificially

Yet another how of giving is 'sacrificially'. Some big men drove up to church in their luxury cars and settled into their nice comfortable seats. When the time came for the offering, they walked purposefully over to the treasury box. Some fished out from their pocket thick wads of notes which they proceeded to put in the treasury box. Others wrote extremely fat cheques. These were generous men. Then a poor old pensioner shuffled past them as they headed back to their seats and put in a few cents. Jesus was watching them and He commented on their giving. According to Him, the old pensioner's offering was the biggest. Her few cents apparently weighed more than the huge sums the rich men gave. I can count, so I might tend to disagree, if I dared. But then Jesus explained further by saying that they had given out of their abundance and she had given all that she had left to live on. That is sacrificial giving. I am struck by the fact that He did not call her foolish; instead, He valued her gift.

This makes me think that there will be times when God will have us give beyond what is naturally convenient for us. The Macedonians who gave to the saints in Jerusalem were not wealthy, but apparently they insisted on being allowed to participate in the privilege of giving and they are said to have given beyond their ability. Note the voluntary nature of their giving. They are not giving under pressure, hoodwinked by the Apostle Paul into parting with their meagre resources. There is no doubt that they must have received an abundant supply based on the principle that Paul enunciated later: those who sow generously will reap generously. No doubt the old widow who gave her mite did not go to sleep hungry either, not when Jesus had witnessed her generosity.

Faithfully

Whatever you do, be faithful. Keep with it, day after day, week after week, month after month. Live a lifestyle of generosity. Whatever other giants you must conquer in your new life in Christ, endeavour to conquer the giant of stinginess. I believe it was John Wesley who said that it would seem that the wallet is the last part of a man to be saved. Bring salvation to your wallet. Jesus made it clear to us that the faithful management of money is a prerequisite in the kingdom of God. In Luke 16.10, we read:

> 'Whoever can be trusted with very little can also be trusted with much, and whosoever is dishonest with very little will also be dishonest with much'.

To whom We Give

All giving is ultimately to God because He is the one who asks us to give. But there are channels for our giving. Jesus said that whatever we did to the least of His brethren, we were doing to Him. When Paul was persecuting the church, Jesus said to him, 'Why do you persecute me?' (Acts 9.4). We give to God through others. These are giving channels. So what are these giving channels?

The Church

The church is working on the earth to advance the purposes of God; consequently, every believer is supposed to participate financially in the work of the church. The saving and discipling of our generation must not suffer for want of resources when God has put resources in the hands of His people for this purpose. Your giving demonstrates your degree of spiritual maturity and vitality.

Ministers of the Gospel

The general feeling in some circles is that a minister of the gospel must live in want to be truly holy. Common sense dictates that a preacher who has difficulty making ends meet will not give the best of themselves; consequently, the believers suffer. The Bible instructs that church leaders must be well taken care of and that they deserve remuneration for the work that they do:

> 'The elders who direct the affairs of the church well are worthy of double honour, especially those whose work is preaching and teaching. For the Scripture says, 'Do not muzzle the ox while it is treading out the grain' and 'The worker deserves his wages' (1 Tim. 5.17-18).

We give so that the church can support the ministers and the leaders.

Furthermore, the individual believer is encouraged to share his prosperity with his spiritual leaders. When a person ministers spiritual, and at times physical life (healing, restoration) to you that enhances your life and brings you blessing, can you go your way enjoying the good things you have without a thought to share them with a person whose intervention was used by God to change your life? *'Anyone who receives instruction in the word must share all good things with his instructor'* (Gal. 6.6).

Poor Believers and the Needy

We have already seen that to watch other believers in need and do nothing to help them is a breach of the law of love. The Apostle James expresses the same idea when he takes to task anyone who sees that a brother or sister has no clothes and no food, and merely tells them to go in peace, be warmed and filled without giving them anything to eat or wear. Your fine words must be backed with action. Giving is action, doing something constructive to solve a person's problem. The book of James is bound to become one of your favourite books of the Bible if you are of a practical mind.

God says that when you have pity on the poor and give them money, it is equivalent to lending to God. Read Proverbs 19.17. You know God is not a debtor. In the same breath He says that God will repay you whatever you have spent on the poor. Conversely, Proverbs 14.31 says that oppressing the poor is reproaching God. We honour God by being gracious to the poor. God's Word even promises that when a person cares for the poor, God will deliver him out of trouble, preserve his life, protect him from his enemies, and heal him.

Benefits of Giving

Benefit One: Your giving is used by God to enrich you

There are rewards for giving. We looked earlier at Jesus' comments on giving and receiving to the effect that when we give, we receive more than we give, in proportion to what we give. Paul said that when you sow generously, you reap generously. Let me quote the rest of Paul's words to the Corinthians:

> 'And God is able to make all grace abound to you, so that in all things at all times, having all that you need, you will abound in every good work. As it is written: "He has scattered abroad his gifts to the poor; his righteousness endures forever." Now he who supplies seed to the sower and bread for food will also supply and increase your store of seed and will enlarge the harvest of your righteousness. You will be made rich in every way so that you can be generous on every occasion, and through us your generosity will result in thanksgiving to God' (2 Corinthians 9.8-11).

As you give, according to this Scripture, God will act on your behalf. He will enable you to have all that you need and you will have more than enough to do good. He will enrich you so you can be continually generous.

Benefit Two: Your giving causes people to pray for you

Not only do people praise God when He uses you to meet their needs, but they also pray for you. And if they cannot pray, someone, somewhere will pray for you. If you give as a lifestyle, imagine what massive impact such prayers will have on your life:

> And in their prayers for you, their hearts will go out to you, because of the surpassing grace God has given you. Thanks be to God for his indescribable gift! (2 Corinthians 9.14-15).

Benefit Three: You enjoy the favour, protection, and provision of God

Several scriptures testify to the fact that God is favourably disposed to those who allow Him to bless others through them, and He moves in their favour. You will enjoy the love of God as God loves a cheerful giver. You will enjoy a high level of protection, preservation from evildoers, physical restoration, and care. God's Word says that is the portion of those who care for the poor. We learn from the example of Paul that when we supply the needs of God's ministers, He supplies our needs. Our finances become His domain. Not that wealth is intrinsically evil, nor that poverty is blessed; rather, obsession with accumulation of wealth is incompatible with devotion to God. God must always be the most important factor in our lives.

Conclusion

This has been one of the most fascinating parts of this book for me. I hope it has been an enjoyable read. Remember, faithfulness in money matters is a qualifier for greater grace. Keep in mind these words of Jesus:

> 'Whoever can be trusted with very little can also be trusted with much, and whoever is dishonest with very little will also be dishonest with much' (Luke 16.10).

Always bear in mind the foundational concept that all things and persons belong to God. You and I belong to God as His creation. We also belong to God as those whom He has redeemed by the precious sacrifice of His Son. The Bible states in First Corinthians Chapter six, verses 19 and 20 that the believer's body is the temple of the Holy Spirit and that he is no longer his own because he was bought with a price. We have become 'a people belonging to God' (1 Peter 2.9). You are God's property, as is all you own. He spoke loudly and clearly in the book of Job, saying,

> 'Who has a claim against me, that I must pay? Everything under heaven belongs to me' (Job 41.11).

He takes out of what He owns and pours out generously on His generous children.

*

Scriptures for meditation

Philippians 4.19 – 'And my God will meet all your needs according to his glorioius riches in Christ Jesus.'

Hebrews 13.5 – 'Keep your lives free from the love of money and be content with what you have, because God has said, "Never will I leave you; never will I forsake you."'

Matthew 6.24 – 'No-one can serve two masters. Either he will hate the one and love the other, or he will be devoted to the one and despise the other. You cannot serve both God and Money.'

1 Timothy 6.17-18 – 'Command those who are rich in this present world not to be arrogant nor to put their hope in wealth, which is so uncertain, but to put their hope in God, who richly provides us with everything for our enjoyment. Command them to do good, to be rich in good deeds, and to be generous and willing to share.'

Psalm 62:10 – '…though your riches increase, do not set your heart on them.'

Proverbs 22.9 – 'A generous man will himself be blessed, for he shares his food with the poor.'

Deuteronomy 16.17 – 'Each of you must bring a gift in proportion to the way the LORD your God has blessed you.'

Luke 12.15 – 'Then he said to them, "Watch out! Be on your guard against all kinds of greed; a man's life does not consist in the abundance of his possessions."'

*

Points to ponder

- All earthly wealth legitimately belongs to God and derives from God, irrespective of how the wealth is brought into the earth and in whose hands it is.
- The shining example of God's giving nature is the giving of His Son; through this most perfect of gifts, eternal life is granted to undeserving sinners.
- God's love is seen in His giving, and so is ours. We thus imitate God by loving and express love by giving. We are not Christ-like until we begin to give.

Discussion questions

1. All wealth belongs to God. How does this affect your perspective of money?
2. Why give?
3. To whom do we give?
4. What is the connection between your generosity and the advancement of the work of the Kingdom?

Prayer

Father, thank You for the grace to give.

I ask that You change me and make me a true and happy giver. Give me seed to sow, I promise to never hold back. I want You to meet needs through me, in Jesus' name, Amen.

10

Change

> "If we desire to walk in the way of the Holy Spirit, we cannot be half hearted or non-commital; we must be prepared to be changed."
>
> Mahesh Chavda
> (The Hidden Power of Speaking in Tongues)

'Do not conform any longer to the pattern of this world, but be transformed by the renewing of your mind. Then you will be able to test and approve what God's will is–his good, pleasing and perfect will' (Romans 12.2).

He has already spent two years behind bars. Now he is summoned before the new governor and the king. They want him to defend himself, yet again, against the accusations levelled at him. Calmly, he speaks in his own defence, recounts his encounter with Jesus, and how his life was radically altered by the commission he then received. He speaks of the before and after, of his obedience to the vision despite opposition from his erstwhile companions whom he had to forsake.

Later on, he would write to his closest associate, one who was like a son to him. He recognised the radical change that had taken place in him. He gave thanks to the Lord because 'he considered me trustworthy, appointing me to his service. Even though I was once a blasphemer and a persecutor and a violent man.' Because he accepted change, Paul the Apostle went from being a murderer to being the strongest voice in Christendom after Christ Himself.

To every one who comes to Christ, the requirement is the same, that, as Paul says before his interrogators, they 'demonstrate their repentance by their deeds' (Acts 26.20). Are we aware that the Bible requires every person who comes to Jesus to undergo change as well? Life in Jesus is a continual process of transformation. We are called to be progressing – becoming better, sweeter, lovelier, and holier in word, thought, and deed. After doing a masterful exposition of the condition of man without God, the saving grace of the gospel, the position of Jews in relation to Christ, the Apostle Paul brings us back to what all of this is meant to lead to in our lives:

> 'Therefore, I urge you, brothers and sisters, in view of God's mercy, to offer your bodies as living sacrifices, holy and pleasing to God – this is your spiritual act of worship. Do not conform any longer to the pattern of this world, but be transformed by the renewing of your mind. Then you will be able to test and approve what God's will is – his good, pleasing and perfect will' (Romans 12.1-2).

It is a firm call to be different from the world, to adopt neither their manner nor their style, to not take on the same colour as the world. But why? Because the moral condition of our world and even our own selves is worse than we imagine. And we serve a holy and pure God.

That is what happened to Eddie. Eddie had been rebellious and violent since childhood. By the time he was fifteen, he had a nasty reputation as a professional thief and had no qualms about stabbing people. One such incident ended in the death of the victim and he was charged with murder, later changed to manslaughter, at age seventeen.

Even in prison, his extreme violence was such that he ended up in a maximum security prison in what he called a prison in a prison. This went on for close to eleven years, a continuous cycle of violence, beatings, and a heart full of hatred and rebellion. Then he began correspondence with some Christians, and God miraculously touched his life. From then on, there was no looking back. He was saved, went through deliverance, and his entire life changed. In his own words, 'I am now placid, peaceful and calm – a happy man. The scowl is gone from my face. The hate is gone from my dark eyes, and now they shine'[1]. Needless to say, it would have been strange to us if, after his encounter with the Lord, he had continued in his old ways.

Change is one of the natural consequences of new birth in Christ. I encourage you to embrace it. You may not have a past as negative as Eddie's. I did not. Yet we all had things in our lives, ways of being and doing that ran counter to God's ways and God's laws. Some of these are glaring; others are more subtle. We must not confuse the fact that God loved us as we were enough to save us with the idea that God wants us to stay the way we are. It is easy for us to see why a violent, condemned criminal needs to change and stop his previous behaviour, isn't it?

Yet we were all moral criminals before God. Allow me to belabour this point. As any pastor can attest, one of the thorniest issues one encounters in ministry is unwillingness

---

1. *When Pigs Move In.* Don Dickerman.

to change. People don't see why. The Apostle writes about our condition prior to faith in Christ as follow:

> 'As for you, you were dead in your transgressions and sins, in which you used to live when you followed the ways of this world and of the ruler of the kingdom of the air, the spirit who is now at work in those who are disobedient. All of us also lived among them at one time, gratifying the cravings of our sinful nature and following its desires and thoughts. Like the rest, we were by nature deserving of wrath' (Eph. 2.1-3).

He further highlights this by noting that, *'Once you were alienated from God and were enemies in your minds because of your evil behaviour'* (Colossians 1.21).

Let's break this down. It says that

- We were dead in our sins
- We used to follow the ways of the world
- We used to be dominated by the devil, the ruler of this world; even as he continues to dominate the disobedient
- We used to gratify ungodly sensual cravings, desires, and thoughts
- We deserved God's anger and judgement
- We were alienated from God
- We were God's enemies

- Our behaviour was evil

In contrast to this, as Ephesians Chapter four puts it, you are *'to live a life worthy of the calling you have received' (v.1)*. For this to take place, change must occur. Back to Romans 12.1 and the injunction to be transformed. The call is for a metamorphosis from the root word 'morphe', meaning 'form'. It is akin, in a sense, to the caterpillar that becomes the butterfly. There is to be a fundamental change of form that proceeds from a deep, inner change in the soul.

I call the Apostle John to the witness stand, and my question is 'What is one to do?' His response: 'Love not the world.'

> 'Do not love the world or anything in the world. If anyone loves the world, love for the Father is not in him. For everything in the world – the cravings of sinful man, the lust of his eyes, and the boasting of what he has and does – comes not from the Father but from the world. The world and its desires pass away, but whoever does the will of God lives for ever' (1 John 2.15-17).

In essence he is saying that there must be a divorce of affections between the believer and the world system. Things we considered normal before must henceforth become strange to us as we cease to love and hold on to them. The challenge we face is that we still have impulses, yearnings and instinctive reactions to these things we are supposed to hate. True, sometimes at conversion, the power of

God so utterly grips some people that they instantly turn their backs on things they used to love and do previously. In some cases people experience a gradual loss of interest. However, change is a process and our willingness to embrace it is vital to its success.

WHERE CHANGE HAPPENS

Our thinking

Change must begin in the mind. Thought patterns, perspectives, and underlying assumptions must be brought under God's scalpel. Before we came to Christ, we were afflicted by what the Bible calls 'futility of (their) thinking', (Ephesians 4.17). Our thoughts were perverse and ungodly. Our values were warped. Our thinking led to words and actions as those described above, actions that characterise the enemies of God.

Now that we are God's friends, we must jettison those thoughts. We must replace them with thinking that honours God, that identifies with His values and that embraces His perspective in all things. The passage we saw in Romans says that as we renew our minds we will be able to ascertain the will of God. God wants you to start seeing things His way rather than seek to convince Him of the rightness or at least the innocuousness of your ways. It is called being in agreement with God.

True symbiosis begins with mind renewal. We are changed. Unrenewed minds oppose the revelation of the

Spirit; they fight the will of God, they oppose the plan of God and impute to God what is not of God.

Our words

Death and life, the Bible says, are in the power of the tongue, (Proverbs 18.21). When we come to the Lord, our tongues must change from being carriers of death to being carriers of life. Not only do your words influence your life, but they also influence other people. Words can cause discouragement, despair, anxiety, rebellion, fear, sin, division, and more. Yet the Bible says that the tongue can also be a tree of life.

Remember what happened when God told Moses He was giving the people the land of Canaan? Moses sent twelve spies into the land to assess it before they went in to fight. Ten of the men came back, and, with their words, painted a picture of such utter helplessness that the people were discouraged. In their despair they spoke of stoning Moses and returning to slavery. They rebelled and God was angry with them. Their punishment was that the entire generation (save Joshua and Caleb, the two remaining spies who spoke with hope and faith in God) would wander forty years in the desert and die there. They would not see the Promised land. None of those people had seen the land before rebelling; they had seen no satellite imagery, no social media pictures. They had heard words and were so affected by them that an entire generation missed its destiny.

Do you know that many churches have been destroyed by believers who could not hold their tongues and chose to spread lies and gossip? Many pastors give up on ministry because they can no longer bear up under the barrage of criticism from within the church and the rebellion stirred up by evil speaking. Some have renounced the call because of verbal abuse.

There is a very interesting passage in the book of James that deals with the power of the tongue and how its significance is inversely proportional to its size. The tongue is a tiny organ, but it directs the course of our lives. James compares it to a rudder that steers a massive ship. The ship goes wherever the rudder leads.

Think about that. Your life goes wherever your tongue leads. What you say will determine what you become and do. Think this through:

> 'If anyone considers himself religious and yet does not keep a tight rein on his tongue he deceives himself and his religion is worthless' (James 1.26).

No wonder there are so many admonitions in the Scriptures about speaking judiciously and in a holy manner. We are enjoined to avoid foolish talk, coarse jesting, slander, gossip, and lies. We are urged to speak in a manner full of grace. We are to speak evil of no one, to avoid quarrelling, to be gentle, and to show perfect courtesy towards all people.

Do you love life and want to have a bright future? Then tame your tongue. 1 Peter 3.10 declares:

> 'For, whoever would love life and see good days, must keep his tongue from evil and his lips from deceitful speech.'

We must no longer speak as casually and glibly as before. We must measure the impact our words have on people. Choose your words wisely to achieve the right effect on people. Let your tongue be a tree of life, not an instrument of death, so you will not be judged severely. The Lord Jesus taught that we will be judged by the words we speak.

Need I say more?

Our actions

'Do ... no more' is a constant exhortation in God's Word. Let him that stole, steal no more, (Ephesians 4.28) for instance. Of all the areas of change, this is the one we are most familiar with. Even then, however, we are not always willing to embrace it. Some of us have been taught that, since we are under grace, our sinful actions have become irrelevant. The blood of Jesus has covered our sins – past, present, and future. What wretched creatures we would be if we received so much yet persisted in wallowing in that which displeases our great and eternal Benefactor? Surely not. Grace empowers us to change; it does not preclude the need for change. Unless we assimilate this, we will balk at change.

Many years ago, a friend who I will call Lara came to faith in Christ. She appeared to be progressing nicely in her faith, but she had concerns. One day, in the course of a conversation, Lara complained that she felt herself becoming different and did not like it. I thought she was changing in all the right ways, but she felt she was losing her personality. She sensed promptings to behave in a gentler, kinder, sweeter manner, which was a total departure from her previously abrasive, somewhat aggressive (albeit often charming) personality. She suddenly felt compunction about saying and doing the things she had previously relished. When she would persist in doing them, remorse would sweep over her. It made her uncomfortable, and she fought it because she did not recognise this new person. She was balking at change.

Do not balk at such change and do not justify sin. If Jesus gave up so much to save you, surely you can give up your sin to honour Him. There is no justification for continuing in wrongdoing when you have committed to follow Jesus. One of the first things you will want to do if you were in the habit of indulging in ungodly conduct with others, is to take a clear stance in dealing with your former companions in iniquity. Let them know the 'party' is over, and that you will no longer be partaking of the devil's delights.

You will need boldness and faith; God will give you both. Initially, your former friends might mock you. Then they will ignore you. Finally, if you continue in the path God has for you, they will come to admire you. What you want to avoid at all costs is trying to placate your friends and family by telling them nothing has changed. In fact, *everything* has changed. What must not change is your love for them; indeed, it must grow stronger. Everything else will separate you now. Your thinking, your words, your deeds will now diverge from their former path.

As to private and personal wrongdoing, confess it to the Lord and tell Him you are done with it. Don't wait for Him to take it away from you or even to take away your desire for it before you stop doing it. Just stop. No matter the pull, decide to not yield.

We obey as a matter of choice, not feeling. Feeling-based obedience is of short duration. The devil will manipulate your feelings to the point where you will do vile things, things that even non-Christians do not do, and feel sorry for yourself to boot. Now if you sense you are under negative spiritual pressure, go to godly elders for deliverance and someone will pray for you. Renounce every occult involvement on your part or by your ancestors and seek freedom from the Lord. The devil does not hold your will captive even though he may oppress you. If he did, you would not have been able to say 'Yes' to the Lord Jesus.

So what we do matters. In fact there are specific things that the Bible tells us that God 'hates'. We must take the decision to stop them.

> 'There are six things that the LORD hates, seven that are detestable to him: haughty eyes, a lying tongue, hands that shed innocent blood, a heart that devises wicked schemes, feet that are quick to rush into evil, a false witness who pours out lies, and a man who stirs up dissension among brothers' (Proverbs 6.16-19).

Change must begin in the mind. Thought patterns, perspectives, and underlying assumptions must be brought under God's scalpel.

THE OBEDIENCE FACTOR

Obedience is a critical dimension of your new life. Obedience is a choice. Resolve to give God unquestioning obedience and unflinching loyalty. It will save your life. You have not become your own man. You have become God's man – to follow Him, honour Him, and serve Him for the rest of your life. It is a high honour. That is why the Scriptures enjoin us to 'live a life worthy of the Lord, and may please him in every way' (Colossians 1:10).

Paul said he was not disobedient to the heavenly vision. It is a fundamental dimension of change. We not only cease to do what is wrong, but we choose to do what is right. Paul ceased killing believers, and he also began to preach the gospel. There is no doubt as to the effectiveness of his work.

God has things in store for you that will alter the trajectory of your life and bring you into a life of fulfilment and effectiveness beyond anything you ever dreamt of. When He speaks, choose to obey. Allow Him to change you, and you will never regret it. You will die happy.

Paul died happy. Towards the end of his life, he wrote to his son in the faith Timothy with these words:

> 'For I am already being poured out like a drink offering, and the time has come for my departure. I have fought the good fight, I have finished the race, I have kept the faith. Now there is in store for me the crown of righteousness, which the Lord, the righteous Judge, will award to me on that day – and not only to me, but also to all who have longed for his appearing' (2 Timothy 4.6-8).

May that be your story. Shalom!

*

Scriptures for meditation

Romans 12.1-2 – 'Therefore, I urge you, brothers, in view of God's mercy, to offer your bodies as living sacrifices, holy and pleasing to God, which is your spiritual act of worship. Do not conform any longer to the pattern of this world, but be transformed by the renewing of your mind. Then you will be able to test and approve what God's will is–his good, pleasing and perfect will.'

Galatians 5.24 – 'Those who belong to Christ Jesus have crucified the sinful nature with its passions and desires.'

Ephesians 4.1-3 – 'As a prisoner for the Lord, then, I urge you to live a life worthy of the calling you have received. Be completely humble and gentle; be patient, bearing with one another in love. Make every effort to keep the unity of the Spirit through the bond of peace.'

Colossians 3.5-10 – 'Put to death, therefore, whatever belongs to your earthly nature: sexual immorality, impurity, lust, evil desires and greed, which is idolatry. Because of these, the wrath of God is coming. You used to walk in these ways, in the life you once lived. But now you must rid yourselves of all such things as these: anger, rage, malice, slander, and filthy language from your lips. Do not lie to each other, since you have taken off your old self with its practices and have put on the new self, which is being renewed in knowledge in the image of its Creator.'

1 John 2.4 – 'The man who says "I know him" but does not do what he commands is a liar, and the truth is not in him.'

*

Points to ponder

- Obedience is a choice. Resolve to give God unquestioning obedience and unflinching loyalty
- Do you love life and want to have a bright future? Then tame your tongue.
- True symbiosis with God begins with mind renewal. An unrenewed mind opposes the revelation of the Spirit, fights the will of God, opposes the plan of God and attributes to God what is not of God.

Discussion questions

1. Why is change important?
2. How does change happen?
3. What are the different areas of change?

Prayer

Father, thank You for the radical change You have produced and are producing in me.

I yield to your Spirit so that He can fine tune me according to your plan and make me as I ought to be. I embrace change, I crave transformation. I accept to renew my mind and to see things your way. Lord, have Your way in my life.

Bibliography

Cowan, Steven B., and Terry L. Wilder. *In Defense of the Bible: A Comprehensive Apologetic for the Authority of Scripture.* N.p.: n.p., n.d. Print.

Cox, John. *Googling God.* Eugene, Or.: Harvest House, 2008. Print.

González, Justo L. *The Story of Christianity.* New York: HarperCollins, 2010. Print.

Hayford, Jack W. *The Beauty of Spiritual Language: A Journey toward the Heart of God.* Dallas: Word Pub., 1992. Print.

Idowu, Moses Oludele. *An Instrument of Revival: The Challenge of Joseph Ayo Babalola, the First Apostle and General Evangelist of the Christ Apostolic Church.* N.p.: n.p., n.d. Web.

McDowell, Josh. *The New Evidence That Demands a Verdict.* Nashville, TN: T. Nelson, 1999. Print.

Orr-Ewing, Amy. *Why Trust the Bible?: Answers to 10 Tough Questions.* Leicester: Inter-Varsity, 2005. Print.

Prince, Derek. *Rediscovering God's Church.* New Kensington, PA: Whitaker House, 2006. Print.

Sheets, Dutch. *Authority in Prayer: Praying with Power and Purpose.* Minneapolis, MN: Bethany House, 2006. Print.

Strobel, Lee. *The Case for Faith: A Journalist Investigates the Toughest Objections to Christianity.* Grand Rapids, MI: ZondervanPublishingHouse, 2000. Print.

About the Author

BOLA OGEDENGBE is the founding pastor of Abba House Church in Paris, France and the founder of The Theophilus Company ministry (La Compagnie Théophile). She worked for many years as a conference interpreter before answering the call to serve God in a full time capacity. She speaks five languages and has a heart for the nations. She has a contagious passion for God, the Gospel and the Person of Christ. The many outreaches of the ministry are geared at winning souls, making disciples and reconciling people to God. Her weekly television programme "Passion pour Dieu" is broadcast worldwide. Many have been blessed by the strong prophetic gift on her life and the deep insights into God's Word she shares in her teachings.

Author's blogs

www.bolaoged.com (English)
www.oliviaoged.com (French)

Other books by Author

REBORN A New Identity

REBORN is a book about the beauty of what God has done for us in the new birth. Everything that the human soul longs and yearns after is offered in salvation, but how little we understand it. REBORN aims to give that understanding. In ten short chapters it captures and paints a magnificent picture of the identity of a person born of God as well as the astounding possibilities that are offered to them. It will make the reader excited about being a Christian, give them greater confidence in the message of the Gospel and empower them to live a God-filled life.

www.ingramcontent.com/pod-product-compliance
Lightning Source LLC
LaVergne TN
LVHW091631070526
838199LV00044B/1022